Praise for

WHY TRAVEL MATTERS

"*Why Travel Matters* is an engaging, intelligent and entertaining exploration of why we travel, how we do it, and what it does to us. I've not read anything like it before. Like the act of travelling itself, it shifted my perspective
on the world and helped me see familiar terrain in unfamiliar ways."   .

Nick Hunt, Author, 2017 FT and Spectator
Book of the Year, *Where the Wild Winds Are*

"Craig Storti has written a highly intelligent and deeply engaging book
that examines not only the beauty but also the importance of travel."

Thomas Swick, Author, *The Joys of Travel:
And Stories That Illuminate Them*

"You may have visited the Taj Mahal and the Great Wall of China, but if
you haven't read this book, you may not have traveled. From deep experience and insight, Craig Storti, with clarity, humor, and a grand sense of
history, shows how travel does matter. In practical steps, he demonstrates
ways we can go beyond mere tourism to become enlightened participants
in new places everywhere. For all travelers—not to mention intercultur-
alists—this book is a must."

Fanchon Silberstein, Former Director,
The Overseas Briefing Center, US Dept. of State.

"Craig Storti compellingly answers the question: 'Why does travel matter?'
He differentiates between travel and tourism, then makes the case that travel
guarantees that the person who set out is not the same one who returns. His
treasury of quotes vividly illuminates his points, adding rich context to this
captivating work. His point: travel is both an inner and outer journey."

Sandra M. Fowler, President, Society of Intercultural
Education, Training, and Research (SIETAR)

Other Works by Craig Storti

Americans at Work: A Guide to the Can-Do People
The Art of Doing Business Across Cultures: 10 Countries,
50 Mistakes, and 5 Steps to Cultural Competence
The Art of Coming Home
The Art of Crossing Cultures
Incident at Bitter Creek: The Story of the Rock
Springs Chinese Massacre
Cross-Cultural Dialogues: 74 Brief Encounters
with Cultural Difference
Old World/New World: Bridging Cultural Differences:
Britain, France, Germany and the U.S.
Speaking of India: Bridging the Communication Gap
When Working with Indians
Understanding the World's Cultures: 20th Anniversary edition of
the classic, *Figuring Foreigners Out*

WHY TRAVEL MATTERS

MATTERS

A Guide to the Life-Changing
Effects of Travel

CRAIG STORTI

NICHOLAS BREALEY
PUBLISHING

BOSTON • LONDON

First published in 2018 by Nicholas Brealey Publishing
An imprint of John Murray Press

An Hachette UK company

23 22 21 20 19 18   1 2 3 4 5 6 7 8 9 10

Copyright © Craig Storti 2018

A CIP catalogue record for this title is available from the British Library.

Library of Congress Control Number: 2017961465

ISBN 978-1-47367-028-0
U.S. eBook ISBN 978-1-47367-030-3
U.K. eBook ISBN 978-1-47367-029-7

Printed and bound in the United States of America.

John Murray Press policy is to use papers that are natural, renewable, and
recyclable products and made from wood grown in sustainable forests.
The logging and manufacturing processes are expected to conform to the
environmental regulations of the country of origin.

John Murray Press Ltd   Nicholas Brealey Publishing
Carmelite House   Hachette Book Group
50 Victoria Embankment   53 State Street
London EC4Y 0DZ   Boston, MA 02109, USA
Tel: 020 3122 6000   Tel: (617) 263 1834

www.nicholasbrealey.com

To Charlotte
for all the places you
have taken me

Contents

Acknowledgments

This book has been over 35 years in the making. I date its inception to 1982, the year I first picked up Paul Fussell's brilliant book, *Abroad: British Literary Traveling between the Wars*. My wife and I were living in England at the time and it was easy to get my hands on all the wonderful writers that book introduced me to. Those writers led me to others, inspiring 35-plus years of reading all the great travel narratives, first the classics that Fussell wrote about and then the more modern travel writers. Along the way I became involved in the intercultural field, which only further fueled my interest in travel literature,

At Nicholas Brealey I would like to thank Alison Hankey, Melissa Carl, and Michelle Morgan, who championed this book as soon as they heard about it. They supported it at every turn, and on occasion even fought for it when necessary. Later in the process, Giuliana Caranante poured her considerable marketing expertise into the book, along with a great deal of personal enthusiasm. Brett Halbleib did an excellent job of copyediting, pulling the book back in several places from the brink of self-indulgence. Two travel writers, Thomas Swick and Nick Hunt, offered great moral support.

Writers erupt in rants from time to time—it's just how they're made—and anyone close to the eruptions can get badly burned. Alison and Michelle felt the heat regularly, and to their credit they never once recoiled. Alas, it's always one's spouse who suffers the worst burns in these cases. I suppose it's all part of the bargain one makes when one marries a writer: close proximity to the occasional crisis of confidence in return for undying gratitude.

Craig Storti

Westminster, MD

Spring 2018

The world is a book and those who do not travel read
only a page.

St. Augustine

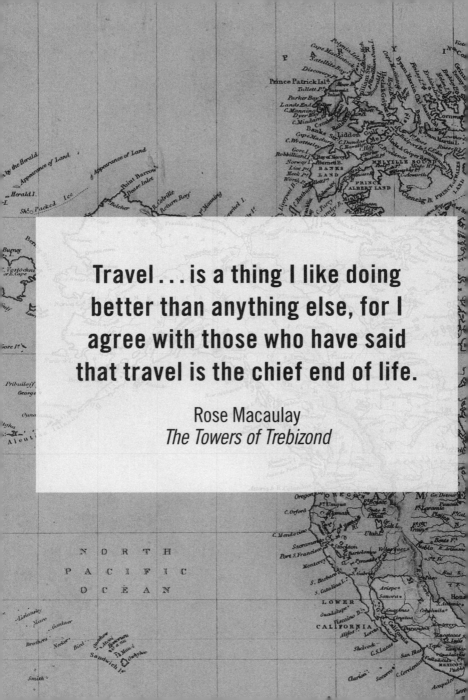

Travel . . . is a thing I like doing better than anything else, for I agree with those who have said that travel is the chief end of life.

Rose Macaulay
The Towers of Trebizond

A Murder in Loughborough

Of the gladdest moments in human life, methinks, is the departure upon a distant journey into unknown lands. Shaking off with one mighty effort the fetters of Habit, the leaden weight of Routine, the cloak of many Cares and the slavery of Home, man feels once more happy. The blood flows with the fast circulation of childhood. Afresh dawns the morn of life.

Richard Burton
The Devil Drives

When you travel, you have a choice: You can be a tourist and have a nice time, or you can be a traveler and change your life. This book is for those who want to change their lives.

For centuries the travel giants—famous travelers and great travel writers—have celebrated the life-altering effects of travel, with its unparalleled opportunities for self-improvement and personal growth.

- "I have a notion that by travel I can add to my personality and so change myself," W. Somerset Maugham wrote. "I do not bring back from a journey quite the same self that I took" (17).
- Alexander Pope wrote that "by travel, generous souls enlarge the mind" (Fussell 1987, 174).
- The 16th-century Chinese traveler Ming-Liao-Tzu declared that he left home "to emancipate his heart and liberate his will" (Zeldin, 307).

This prospect of a life-changing experience informs all the classic phrases used to describe the impact of travel, that it broadens your horizons, changes your perspective, deepens your understanding, that travel opens you up. But while all these things *can* happen when you travel, there are no guarantees.

This book is for those who would like to know more about the opportunities travel offers and how to make the most of them. It is for those who would like to add to their personality, enlarge their mind, and bring back a different self from the one who set out. It is for those who want to learn what travel has to teach. Such a person in these pages is known as a serious traveler.

To be sure these phrases come easily: broaden your horizons, change your perspective, add to your personality. But what do they mean? How exactly is a person who has had his* horizons broadened different from someone who has not? What are the precise mechanisms by which travel accomplishes these marvelous transformations? And most importantly, what does the traveler have to

---

* Throughout the text, the pronouns "he" and "she" are used in alternate chapters to refer to the traveler in third person singular.

do to make sure the self he brings back is not the same one he left home with? These are the questions that inspired this book and that will be answered in these pages.

There are those, let's call them the travel purists, who would consider this entire undertaking a fool's errand. Because travel, you see, is dead. It was killed off years ago by tourism. You can still journey to distant shores, of course, but the purists insist that you can no longer travel.

And these people certainly know whereof they speak. They can tell you the identity of the man who killed travel, the date of its demise, the scene of the crime, the murder weapon, the number of witnesses, and even the name of the principal accomplice. The perpetrator was the businessman Thomas Cook, the date was July 5, 1841, the place was the Loughborough train station in the British Midlands, the weapon was a train ride, there were 570 witnesses, and Cook's partner in crime was none other than George Pullman, the inventor of the Pullman railroad car.

So what exactly happened at Loughborough on that fateful day? Cook had persuaded officials of the Midland Counties Railway to offer a reduced fare for one of the trips along their line, the 15-mile journey from Loughborough to Leicester, in return for a guarantee of a sizeable number of passengers. The officials agreed, and in the end Cook turned out 570 "excursionists," all members of the Harborough Temperance Society and sister organizations en route to their regional meeting in Leicester. "This excursion proved so popular," Lynne Withey writes in her history of leisure travel, "that Cook kept himself busy over the next three summers organizing trips for Temperance Society Members and Sunday school children throughout the region" (136).

And Cook never looked back. Over the next few years, he arranged longer and longer excursions, first within the UK and later to continental Europe. Cook's tours, as they came to be known, introduced four new elements to the experience of travel— speed, comfort, convenience, and the tour group—and in the process created what we would now call tourism, a highly sanitized, worry-free kind of travel, carefully scrubbed of any experiences that might unsettle, disturb, or confuse the tourists or otherwise strike them dumb. "The man who started the rot," John Julius Norwich writes,

> was that disagreeable old abstainer Thomas Cook, who, already by the middle of the century, had developed the idea of insulating his clients as far as possible from the uncouth conditions all too frequently prevailing in foreign parts by swathing them in a protective cocoon of block bookings [and] meal vouchers. (1)

For all intents and purposes, it was travel without foreigners. Over time, tourism became the preferred way to travel for millions of people, and it has continued to thrive down to the present day.

If we're being fair, we can't really say travel was murdered that day in Loughborough, the day tourism was born, but it was certainly wounded and definitely diminished. Travel had to swallow its pride after Loughborough, and from that day forward it was obliged to compete with tourism to capture the hearts and minds of all those who went abroad. But as we will see in these pages, so long as the essential ingredients of true travel still exist—an unfamiliar place, its unfamiliar inhabitants, and a curious observer— then the possibility of travel will always be with us. And so long as travel is still possible, then horizons can still be broadened, hearts can still be emancipated, and minds can still be enlarged.

Tourism did not kill travel that day in the British Midlands, then; it simply made it more difficult, throwing up numerous obstacles and temptations that the serious traveler of today must be aware of and try to avoid. In short, those who venture abroad today must make a conscious choice: to be a tourist or to be a traveler.

If you'd like to change your life, then be a traveler.

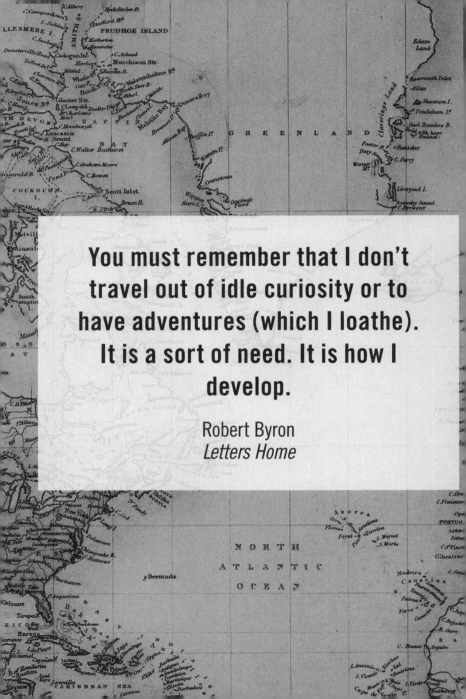

You must remember that I don't travel out of idle curiosity or to have adventures (which I loathe). It is a sort of need. It is how I develop.

Robert Byron
Letters Home

CHAPTER 1

Why Travel Matters

The goal in these pages is twofold: to describe the life-altering effects of travel (chapters 1–4) and to explain how to have the kind of journey that will indeed change your life (chapter 5). We will take up those topics presently but we should first define what we mean by travel, both in the modern era generally and in these pages in particular.

Our subject here is travel to a foreign country and a different culture, not travel inside our own country. Most contemporary observers and scholars of travel agree on the ingredients that define "true" or "serious" travel (so-called because there is also recreational or leisure travel, otherwise known as tourism), and they likewise agree that it's important to distinguish between travel and tourism. Not so much because one is superior to the other but because they are different kinds of experience with very different results, and people should choose the experience that will give them the results they're looking for.

Tourism is largely *escape from* whereas true travel is *arriving at*; tourism is mainly recreational whereas travel is primarily educational; tourists are driven around and served by the locals whereas travelers want to meet them; tourists want to relax whereas travelers want to be stimulated; the goal of tourism is to see the sights, while the goal of travel is to add to understanding. Paul Theroux, in his trademark curmudgeon mode, observed that "travelers don't know where they're going [because that's not the point] and tourists don't know where they've been" (Swick, 7). In *The Oxford Book of Exploration* Robin Hanbury-Tenison makes his own sharp distinctions: "There are tourists and there are travellers. The former go abroad to rest their bodies and their minds, no more. The latter go to see and understand" (xiv).

We define travel herein as *journeying to a foreign country and encountering a different culture for the purpose of personal growth and self-improvement*. Or, as W. Somerset Maugham would have it: adding to one's personality and bringing back a different self.

But travel in this sense and to these ends has not existed for most of human history, not until the last 300 years or so. Understanding how travel has evolved through the ages will put in perspective the unique opportunities travel offers in the present era. And that perspective, in turn, may inspire today's voyagers to seize these rare opportunities and make the most of their journeys—inspire them, in short, to be travelers rather than tourists. To that end we take a few pages to offer a short biography of travel.

A Brief History of Travel

Ever since humans graced the earth, more than two million years ago, we have been nomadic wanderers.... Sedentary lifestyles in which people sat around log

fires until the cows came home are as fictional as they
are absurd. Humans don't do it. They have to travel.

Christopher Lloyd

At the dawn of history the human condition was nothing *but*
travel, in the sense of moving about or nomadism. The life of the
hunter-gatherer, the lot of humanity for close to two million years,
was ceaseless movement, following the herds and the seasons. If
there had been a word for travel back at the dawn of human history, it would have been the equivalent of the word for "life," or
"existence," or "the way things are," or simply "what we do."

"Survival depended on mobility and opportunism," Brian
Fagan has written of the Late Ice Age (16,000 to 13,000 BC). "It
was a world of small-scale living, of widely cast social networks,
of occasional gatherings where several bands came together, but,
above all, of mobility, where small groups survived by ranging over
enormous territories..." (29). This was movement, to be sure, but
personal growth was certainly not the object.

Many observers cite the primordial preeminence of nomadism to explain our puzzling 21st-century wanderlust, to account,
that is, for the call of the road enduring into the modern era, long
past the time when travel was necessary. If we consider how long
mankind spent as wanderers, close to two million years, compared
to how long we have lived in towns and villages, less than 20,000
years, it's no wonder we feel like taking a trip every so often just
for the fun of it. Wandering is in our DNA, much like the human
fascination with fire. A French writer, Gontran de Poncins, once
asked an Eskimo why his people were always on the move. "What
can we do?" the man replied. "We are born with the great unrest"
(*Washington Post Book World*, 14).

Then somewhere between 8,000 and 15,000 years ago, mankind learned how to domesticate and breed certain animals and how to grow certain crops, and human history changed forever. Along with the dawn of agriculture came the birth of sedentism, the habit of staying in place, and the beginning of semi- and ultimately permanent settlements. It became normal *not* to move about or regularly change one's location, and as sedentism and staying put became the norm, nomadism and travel became the exception.

And not merely the exception: travel quickly became decidedly dangerous and hence demonstrably unwise. To be on the road (although there were almost no roads as such at this time) inevitably meant that you were separated from a settlement and no longer belonged to or could count on the protection and goodwill of a permanent kinship group. You were an exile, a stranger, and there was no one to protect the stranger, no one whose interests were allied with those of the stranger, no one who would benefit in any way from extending courtesy or goodwill to the stranger. If you were on the road in the Stone Age or the Bronze Age, it was because others had ordained it, and they would only ordain such a thing if your presence among them was undesirable. You were on the road, in short, because you had been deemed unfit to inhabit home.

One of Christianity's great foundation stories, the tale of Adam and Eve, is an allegory of this momentous shift in the human condition from nomadism to sedentism. The story of Adam and Eve is first and foremost a cautionary tale, extolling the virtues of being settled and, largely by implication, the dangers of wandering. The Garden of Eden, after all, is the epitome of sedentism, with its self-reproducing abundance of foodstuffs and its tame and obedient animals. For their sins, Adam and Eve are banished from this idyllic world and condemned to wander. The moral of the tale is clear: only the foolish would risk the refuge and protection offered by the settled life. And the punishment for such foolishness—in Biblical parlance, Adam and Eve's "penance"—is travel. Thus did travel or nomadism morph from being the human condition to being anathema.

In his book *The Mind of the Traveler*, Eric Leed observes that the oldest source of our word *travel* is probably the Indo-European root *per*, "many of the secondary meanings of which refer explicitly to motion: 'to cross space,' 'to reach a goal,' 'to go out'" (5). And the primary meanings of *per*—to try, to test, to risk—are where we get our words *experiment* and *peril*. Paul Fussell finds another and more recent ancestor in the word *travail*. "A traveler is one who suffers travail," he writes, "a word deriving in its turn from Latin *tripalium*, a torture instrument consisting of three stakes designed to rack the body" (1980, 39).

Homer's *Odyssey* is probably the most famous example of the Bronze Age view of travel as deeply undesirable, an ordeal, a series of trials that the hero must somehow survive. Odysseus neither chooses to be a traveler nor actively seeks adventure; he is shipwrecked on his return from the Trojan wars and is simply trying to get back to his homeland, Ithaca, and to his beloved wife, Penelope, as soon as possible. Fortunately for western literature, it takes him ten years. From Odysseus' perspective, his epic adventures are only so many unwanted obstacles to overcome, so many tests set by the gods to keep him from the bosom of home. "There is nothing worse for mortals," Homer writes, "than a wandering life" (Lapham, 52).

Notice, also, how that other great traveler of the Bronze Age, Gilgamesh, likewise finds his path strewn with obstacles he must surmount before he can return home to his capital, Uruk. "He had journeyed to the edge of the world," his epic story begins, "and made his way back, exhausted but whole. He had carved his trials on stone tablets" (Mitchell, 69). "Trials," they are called, not adventures. "When we think of travel in the remote past," Peter Whitfield has observed,

> a number of powerful and resonant words come into our minds: Exodus and Odyssey, Epic and Saga, Quest and Pilgrimage. Each of these words has its own distinct meaning, but all convey one of the primal senses of travel—that it was an ordeal, a challenge, an experience to be endured. Travel was associated with suffering. (2)

Travel in the Stone, Bronze, and Iron Ages, then, is mostly trials, obstacles, and perils. The traveler is not so much a hero as someone to be pitied, and accordingly the arc of the travel narrative is always homeward. Travel is not a journey outward, *from* home, but the return voyage *to* home.

One way or another this state of affairs continued through ancient times, up through the Dark Ages and to the beginning of the Middle Ages. By this time strangers no longer had the roads to themselves, of course, but the three most common types of travelers during these epochs—soldiers (including sailors), merchants or traders, and pilgrims—were certainly not in search of self-improvement. Pilgrims probably came the closest, but even pilgrims did not travel for personal growth but to save their immortal souls. "There is plenty of movement from place to place," Paul Fussell has written of travel in the ancient world and the Dark Ages, but for there to be "real travel, movement from one place to another should manifest some impulse of non-utilitarian pleasure.... Until then, it is perhaps best to speak not of travel but of pre-travel" (1987, 21).

By the early Middle Ages there were many more roads and many more people on them. "On the main highways," medieval historian Morris Bishop has observed, "the traffic was very heavy." But there was still no one we would call a traveler.

> Everyone was on the roads: monks and nuns on errands for their community; bishops bound for Rome or making a parochial visitation; wandering students; singing pilgrims following their priests and their banners; papal postmen; minstrels, quacks, and drug sellers; chapmen and tinkers; seasonal workmen and serfs out of bond; discharged soldiers, beggars, and highwaymen.... (185, 186)

In his book *Touring in 1600*, E. S. Bates summarizes the reasons the wise stayed close to home during the 16th and 17th centuries.

> The roads were dangerous, the inns wretched, the ships unseaworthy, the maps so bad as to be seen as gifts to an enemy rather than to a friend.... Never journey without something to eat in your pocket, if only to throw to dogs when attacked by them, and if bringing a watch, make sure it was not a striker, for that warns the wicked you have cash (Lapham, 15).

Waiting for the Self

> [C]onventions of self-consciousness and inward scrutinizing [were] not common much before the Renaissance and not highly developed until people in the

later eighteenth century became obsessed with "personality."

Paul Fussell
The Norton Book of Travel

Travel for the sake of self-improvement requires a self, and most observers agree that the self did not make its appearance in the world until the late Middle Ages. There were individuals long before the Renaissance, of course, but there was not *individualism* as we know it today. This is difficult for modern man to grasp since individualism is such a fundamental part of the contemporary notion of identity. Indeed, the very phrase we use to describe identity—self-concept—is not even imaginable absent the notion of individualism. The idea that there could have been something *before* the self, a way of being that did not somehow encompass the notion of personal identity, is almost impossible to get our modern minds around.

So if these pre-moderns didn't look upon themselves as individuals, just who did they think they were? They were the children of God, to begin with, created in His image and put on earth to serve, worship, and obey Him. The core of their being was their connection to the divine. The human condition was widely regarded as "nasty, brutish, and short," as Thomas Hobbes reminded us—very short in the Middle Ages—and anyway, life wasn't the main event. What really mattered was the *after*life. "To true Christians," William Manchester observes, "life on Earth was almost irrelevant. During it they obeyed the precepts of Catholicism to safeguard their future in paradise. The thought of living for the sheer sake of living, celebrating mortal existence before God took them unto his own, was subversive of the entire [religious] structure" (113).

Nor was individualism encouraged by the harsh circumstances of daily life before the late Middle Ages. Subsistence living was the norm, and for most people it was only possible via communal arrangements. Kin and clan were everything, and the group was the only viable unit of survival. The well-being of the group always came first, thereby offering a modicum of safety and security to its individual members.

In *A World Lit Only by Fire,* William Manchester observes that most people in the Middle Ages did not even have names, the ultimate signifier of self, since there was no need. "Noblemen had surnames," he writes, "but fewer than one percent of the souls in Christendom were wellborn. [For] the rest...a nickname would do. Because most peasants lived and died *without ever leaving their birthplace*, there was seldom need for any tag beyond One-Eye, or Roussie (Redhead), or Biona (Blondie), or the like" (21; italics added).

The secular world, then, much like the spiritual one, offered precious little scope for the emergence of the individual and the possibility of self-expression. "The most baffling, elusive, yet in many ways most significant dimension of the medieval mind," Manchester continues, "was the medieval man's total lack of ego. Even those with creative powers had no sense of self.... Their anonymity approached the absolute. So did their mute acceptance of it" (21, 22).

The Birth of Individualism

> A basic psychological change, a certain form of *individuality,* was born in Europe some time between 1000 and 1200, and [this] accounts most of all for the Western mentality.
>
> Peter Watson
> *Ideas: A History of Thought and Invention*

And then, sometime in the late Middle Ages, all this began to change: A fundamental realignment of human aspiration and interest took place, away from a preoccupation with God and the next life to a focus on man and the present life. Such a momentous shift had a number of causes, but one of the most significant was the rediscovery of the classic Greek thinkers and philosophers, especially Aristotle, and with it the restoration of logic and reason to compete with revelation and faith. "A secular way of thinking was introduced into the world," Peter Watson writes, "which would eventually change man's understanding for all time" (331).

Martin Luther greatly abetted the cause of individualism at this crucial juncture by challenging the infallibility of the Catholic church and church teaching. If Rome was not all-knowing, then man would have to decide for himself what to believe and what not to believe (guided, of course, by the Bible). Still, the idea was now out there that the individual was much more of a player in his or her life than ever before.

The printing press was yet a third midwife at the birth of individualism by putting books—hence knowledge—within the reach of more and more people. Those who could read, and their number was growing during the late Middle Ages, could now educate themselves and not have to rely on the church to tell them what was true and what was not. Luther's apostasy and the almost simultaneous spread of the written word forever robbed the church of its monopoly on knowledge and its stranglehold on truth. People could make their own inquiries into the nature of reality and decide for themselves what was true. By the advent of the Renaissance (the early 1400s), the individual, who had been stirring for two centuries all over Europe, was increasingly restless and on the verge of standing up.

'The man of the Renaissance lived, as it were, between two worlds," Watson writes:

> He was suspended between faith and knowledge. As the grip of medieval supernaturalism began to loosen, secular and human interests became more prominent. The facts of individual experience here on earth became more interesting than the shadowy afterlife. Reliance on God and faith weakened. The present world became an end in itself instead of a preparation for a world to come. (398)

The Coming of Travel

> Where one Englishman traveled in the reign of the first two Georges, ten now go on a grand tour.
>
> Anonymous (1772)

The arrival of the individual on the stage of history by the end of the 1400s did not turn people into true or serious travelers overnight; it turns out that the concept of self was a necessary but not a sufficient condition for the emergence of true travel. Several other elements were still needed: good roads, a means of conveyance, money, and, most important, leisure time.

We've already noted that until the later Middle Ages most roads were poorly maintained or not maintained at all and not especially safe. Moreover, most roads in Europe did not have signposts at crossroads until the last decades of the 1600s; clearly, roads were used primarily by people who already knew the way and not by strangers passing through. And even if there had been good, safe, and signposted roads, the means to travel—a horse, a wagon, a boat, or, later, a coach or carriage—were beyond the resources of all but traders and the very rich, both of whom did in fact take to the roads in great numbers during the Middle Ages. If you had to travel, you walked, but then you needed money for food and a bed whenever you broke your journey, and disposable income was likewise beyond the means of all but the elite.

But for most people the missing ingredient, the one thing that might otherwise have caused their minds to turn towards travel, was the lack of leisure time. The common man and woman of the Middle Ages and the Renaissance did not have whole days and weeks free to do nothing but take to the roads. Subsistence living was the lot of the majority, and it did not allow for time off, except perhaps in the coldest part of the winter, when no one traveled who did not absolutely have to.

Most observers agree that travel as we know it today, travel to see the world, began in the 16th century in Europe, with what was called the "grand tour." The grand tour was "a distinctly modern phenomenon," Lynne Withey observes, reaching

> its heyday in the late eighteenth [century]. Although limited mainly to the sons of wealthy families and intended primarily for educational purposes, by the middle of the eighteenth century the grand tour had become common enough among Britain's upper classes, and combined pleasure and instruction to such an extent, that it constitutes the first significant example of leisure travel on a large scale. (x)

The grand tour originally took in northern Europe—France, Germany, the Netherlands, Switzerland—along with Spain and Italy. But before long it was covering most of the Mediterranean, including Greece and Turkey. And then it became even grander, with scions of the best families regularly turning up in Egypt and the Holy Land.

The express purpose of the grand tour was very close to the modern travel goal of self-development. The point was to complete one's formal education (which emphasized the classics) by visiting the "cradle of civilization" as it was called, the famous locations of antiquity—Greece, Turkey (for Troy), and Rome—and also to see first-hand the wonders of the Renaissance. For young men of means and ambition (the tour was largely a male phenomenon until the 19th century), the grand tour was a box that needed to be checked off on their rise to power and influence.

In *Travel: A Literary History*, Peter Whitfield notes that at this point travel was no longer just a

> realm of action, not an incidental factor in military campaigning, in pilgrimage or in trade, but an intellectual force which had reshaped man's understanding of his world. Travel would increasingly become a realm of thought, an experience which led to re-evaluations of the world and of the traveler's own personality. (63)

The coming of the railroads revolutionized travel and soon brought it within reach even of the working class, thanks mainly to the efforts of the English businessman Thomas Cook. As we have seen, Cook organized his first train excursion in the summer of 1841 from Loughborough to Leicester, a journey of 15 miles, for a group of temperance society members. It was quite an event: a brass band played at the train station, and there were nearly as many curious spectators on hand as there were excursionists. A year later Cook organized his first tour to Scotland, and by the time of the Paris Exhibition of 1855, he was regularly sending his countrymen and women off to continental Europe.

The grand tour and Thomas Cook were the last two steps in travel's long journey to modernity, and in Cook's case, the first step in travel's transformation into tourism. The grand tourists are the first travelers in which we moderns can easily recognize our own traveling selves. Indeed, we might even have been on that platform at Loughborough, not to attend a temperance meeting, of course, but eager to see the wider world and add to our personality.

The End of Travel?

> I am assuming that travel is now impossible and that tourism is all we have left.
>
> Paul Fussell
> *Abroad: British Literary Traveling*
> *between the Wars*

Scholars of travel have not been kind to Thomas Cook, seeing his tours as the beginning of the end of travel and the start of the age of tourism. While Cook should not be blamed for the excesses of his many imitators, it is true, as we will see in the following chapters, that the four elements Cook et al. introduced to the travel experience—speed, comfort, convenience, and the tour group— are the hallmarks of tourism and the sworn enemies of true or serious travel. "We go abroad," Frederic Harrison wrote, " but we travel no longer" (Fussell, 1980, 41). And he wrote that in 1887.

Cook introduced group travel, which soon evolved into mass travel and then quickly became tourism, as more and more groups took to the roads. In group travel, one spends most of one's time with one's fellow travelers, almost never meets a local (or at least none who don't speak one's native tongue), stays and eats in hotel chains imported from one's home country, and travels in glass-covered, air-conditioned buses from which one peers out at and photographs what are known as "the sights." There is only the most fleeting contact with the place and virtually none with its inhabitants, except for waiters and tour guides. It is what Paul Fussell calls "the calculated isolation from the actual" (1980, 44). George Orwell was less polite in a letter he wrote from Marrakech to a friend in England, referring to tourists as "the bastards who travel...from hotel to hotel, never seeing any difference anywhere except in the temperature" (Fleming, 342).

Paul Fussell was a brilliant thinker, a beautiful stylist, an unrivaled expert on travel—and something of a curmudgeon. He held out little hope for travel in the age of tourism, but even he agreed that "what distinguishes the tourist is the motives," suggesting the possibility that with the right motives perhaps travel might still be attainable.

And one of Fussell's very few rivals, in erudition in general and in the lore of travel in particular (and, like Fussell, the editor of an anthology of travel writing), John Julius Norwich is actually quite hopeful about the possibility of travel at the present time. Writing about some of the long-dead contributors to his anthology, he noted that

> the overwhelming majority of the contributors to this volume had no choice in the matter. For them tourism did not exist; you were a traveler or you were a stay-at-home, and that was that. As to the remainder, they were—or in some cases still are—travelers because that is what they were determined to be from the start, and they have taught us

a vitally important lesson: that we can all still be travelers rather than tourists if we set our minds to it.... The difference today lies less in the places we go to than in the way in which we go to them; it is perfectly possible to be a traveler in France—or even in England, for that matter—just as it is to be a tourist on the Upper Amazon. (3)

If scholars agree that travel today is not nearly as easy as it once was, challenged at every turn by the appeal of tourism, then this brief history offers hope, showing how all those contemporary challenges notwithstanding, travel has now evolved to the point where it promises rewards beyond anything previously imaginable. In the pages to come we will describe these riches and offer suggestions for how you can claim them. All you will have to do is follow Norwich's advice and "set [y]our mind to it."

Travel and Experience

Travel must be "experience" at its highest.
Louis MacNeice
Autumn Journal

Now that we've brought travel into the 21st century, it's time to take up our central theme in these pages: the effects of travel and how travel achieves those effects. This means it's time to talk about experience—*new* experience, to be more precise—since the true significance of travel and the source of all its effects is the fact that travel by its very nature is mankind's greatest source of new experiences. New experiences and what they lead to are why travel matters.

What Is Experience?

> He knew nothing yet well enough to see it. You cannot
> see things until you know roughly what they are.
> C. S Lewis
> *Out of the Silent Planet*

To understand the significance of new experience, we first need to understand what experience is and the role it plays in our mental development. Simply stated, experience is what happens when the external world meets the internal one, when the material world outside ourselves makes contact with "us," the interior world that we think of as our mind, consciousness, or self. This contact occurs when elements of the external world impinge on any one of our five senses: sight, sound, smell, taste, or touch. What we think of as our senses are in fact a collection of receptors that receive a series of impressions from the objects that stimulate them. These impressions are then sent on to the relevant parts of the brain that processes them, receiving, encoding, and storing this raw input in a vast data bank we usually refer to as our sensory memory.

"Our senses are the gateways between our brain and the outside world," Barry Gibb has written. "Most of our memories are based on sensory input. But what is memory? It's the brain's ability to encode, store, and retrieve thoughts and sensory experiences" (45, 63). Memory enables perception, and perception is how we see, hear et cetera. Using the sense of sight as our principal example, notice what happens when we "see" something.

"The eyes are given altogether too much credit for seeing," Frank Smith has written.

The eyes do not see at all, in a strictly literal sense. The eyes *look*, they are devices for collecting information for the brain, largely under the direction of the brain, and it is the brain that determines what we see and how we see it. The brain's perceptual decisions are based only partly on information from the eyes, *greatly augmented by information that the brain already possesses.* (25; italics added)

You don't see what is in front of you, in short; you see your brain's perception—its reconstruction—of what is in front of you, created with matches the brain retrieves from previously stored visual input.

This describes what happens when you see something you have seen before, something the brain has a visual memory of (what Smith calls the "information that the brain already possesses"). But what happens when you see something you've never seen before, such as all those new sense impressions that bombard you when you travel? For the most part, the same process unfolds, only with a different end result. Your sense receptors still receive the impressions from the external object, still send those impressions on to the brain, and the brain still goes looking in your memory for matches, preparing to construct an image or visual perception for you.

But in the case of something you have never seen before, the brain draws a blank; it doesn't find any matches. "Sight fails," Simon Hoggart writes, "when presented with something it has never formerly seen" (*Spectator*, 62). Undaunted, the brain does the best it can under the circumstances and presents you with the closest matches it can find. What you perceive in that case is not precisely what you have in front of you but the brain's closest visual memory—its best guess—at what you have in front of you.

This is the principle (and the science) behind most optical illusions, wherein the brain is tricked into seeing things that aren't really there, as in the example (one of the famous Kanizsa triangles) reprinted on the next page.

When you first look at this image, you probably see three small triangles and a large white one, whereas in fact there are no triangles, nothing with three lines enclosing a space, anywhere in this image. There are three Pac-Man-like shapes, three V-shaped objects, and nothing else. But the brain "sees" the triangles in this drawing because when it searches your visual memory for matches to this particular set of visual impressions, all previous experiences of images like this involved triangles, so that's what the brain shows you.

"[T]he brain's eagerness to find shapes," Matthew MacDonald writes of this image in *Your Brain: The Missing Manual,*

> leads it to find shapes where there aren't any.... An arrangement [of shapes] like this *would be unlikely in the natural world*, so your brain quickly dismisses that possibility... picks up on a few clues and performs a rapid analysis to determine the *most likely* explanation. (83; italics added)

In short, the brain can't see—and can't show you—what it has never seen before. But as you look at the drawing longer, and the brain starts to receive and encode some impressions that do *not* depict a triangle, *these* impressions are added to your visual memory, so that eventually it is an image without any triangles—that is, the actual drawing—that the brain will be able to retrieve and present to you. Note how it is these new sense impressions, the results of *new experience*, that eventually make it possible for you to construct an accurate perception and see the image as it really is.

Here are two examples of this phenomenon from my own experience. I was once flying over Greenland, looking down on it from 35,000 feet, and I saw some objects in the ocean and decided they must be a series of tall, sheer rock outcroppings. Then, as we got further away from land and the objects were still there, I concluded these couldn't be outcroppings that far out into the ocean, so then they became massive whitecaps. Finally, when the whitecaps weren't moving, I concluded the objects must be icebergs, which is what they were.

I had never seen icebergs before, not from above, anyway, so for the first few milliseconds of this experience, these objects were not icebergs; that is, my brain could not present icebergs to my vision because it had no relevant visual data to work with. So it came up with its best guess: rock outcroppings. When that did not reflect reality, my brain tried again and came up with another phenomenon one frequently finds in oceans (and therefore has visual memory of): large whitecaps. All the while, of course, my brain was encoding and storing the new sense impressions it was receiving from these strange objects, and finally it had enough visual memory to construct and present to me an image of icebergs.

A similar thing happened once to an English companion of

mine when we were on a golf course outside Nairobi. A monkey darted out of the woods onto the fairway and ran off with the Englishman's golf ball. "What's that badger doing with my golf ball?" he cried. This man almost certainly knew what a monkey was and obviously knew about fairways and golf balls, but as he had never seen them in the same image before, his brain searched his visual memory bank and came up empty-handed. And then proceeded to do the best a British brain could under the circumstances—and presented the man with a badger.

Philip Glazebrook, in his delightful *Journey to Kars*, tells the story of two 19th-century "nervous clergymen" traveling in the Balkans

> on a Danube steamer [who] reported to the papers dreadful atrocities on every hand, a perfect forest of Bulgar Christians impaled on stakes as far as the eye could see. And much fury against the Turk was expended until it was pointed out that the 'Christians' were more probably bundles of fodder spiked up out of reach of the stock, as had been the Balkan way of doing the thing for any number of centuries. (198)

New Experiences

> He gazed about him, and the very intensity of his desire to take in the new world at a glance defeated itself. He saw nothing but colors—colors that refused to form themselves into things.
>
> C. S. Lewis
> *Out of the Silent Planet*

Clearly the brain processes new, unfamiliar input differently from old, familiar input. When the brain sees what it has seen before, it finds matches quickly, and you see things immediately. With unfamiliar objects, the brain searches far and wide for matches, and this prolonged search takes time and effort. "The more alternatives the brain has to consider and discard," Frank Smith says of this process, "the longer it takes the brain to make up its mind, so to speak, and for seeing to occur" (31). And with unfamiliar objects, meanwhile, the brain is not only looking everywhere for matches, it is also busy encoding and storing the new input from your sense receptors to create new visual memory.

This difference in the time it takes the brain to "see" the familiar and the unfamiliar explains the experience we have all had of taking a trip—driving, let's say—to an unfamiliar destination and then driving back the way we came. One always has the impression that the return journey is much faster than the outward journey. In actual fact, the two trips take the same amount of real (objective) time, assuming similar traffic conditions and driving speeds, but the outward journey seems longer because the brain is going into overtime processing all the new visual stimuli. On the return journey, however, the brain has seen many of these sights before, albeit from a different direction, and can produce them much more quickly. Cognizing always takes more time (more processing) than *re*cognizing. To put it another way, while the objective or real time of both trips is in fact the same, the subjective time—how long the trip *feels* to us—is shorter on the way back because the brain doesn't have to work as hard.

The extra time and effort it takes for the brain to process unfamiliar objects explain a number of things that happen when we travel and are bombarded with new input. This extra effort explains the common feeling of being overwhelmed that many travelers experience, especially at the start of a journey. Different travelers describe the phenomenon differently—as "sensory overload," or a feeling that it's all "too much," or, in the vernacular, that it's "mind-blowing"—but in the end it all comes down to the same thing: overstimulation. Processing the almost continuous succession of new sense impressions sends the brain into serious overdrive.

"What can I say about it all?" The novelist Gustave Flaubert wrote his sister soon after arriving in Egypt.

What can I write you? As yet I am scarcely over the initial bedazzlement. It is like being jerked while still asleep into the midst of a Beethoven symphony, with the brasses at their most ear-splitting, the basses rumbling, and the flutes sighing away; each detail reaches out to grip you; it pinches you; and the more you concentrate on it the less you grasp the whole. Then gradually all this becomes harmonious and the pieces fall into place of themselves, in accordance with the laws of perspective. But the first days, by God, it is such a bewildering chaos of colors that your poor imagination is dazzled as though by continuous fireworks. (Steegmuller, 79)

The fact that the brain presents you initially with approximate and only later with exact matches of the external world explains why we don't see many things very clearly or completely the first few hours in an unfamiliar environment. Since the brain cannot retrieve from your visual memory what it has not previously stored there, since it cannot _re_cognize what it has never cognized in the first place, the brain only sees what it has already seen. An Arab probably sees something more akin to a minaret when she first gazes upon the Gothic spires of a French cathedral, while a French traveler sees something closer to a Gothic spire when she gets her first look at a minaret. This same phenomenon also explains why we keep seeing new things in our surroundings the longer we spend in them; as the brain completes its encoding of new input, adding the results to our visual memory, it is able to find and retrieve images closer and closer to the reality before our eyes.

Many travelers have remarked on this phenomenon of being unable to actually see what they are looking at. As Edmond Taylor observes in his book *Richer By Asia*,

> It is one of my regrets that I have not yet learned to see an Indian village or a bazaar; my eyes aren't trained, and I couldn't describe one to save my life. I love them and am endlessly fascinated; but all I can make out is a wild surrealist confusion of men and animals and many kinds of inanimate objects, arranged in completely implausible patterns. (17)

"I wish my eyes were better able to see the differences," J. G. Farrell writes in *Indian Diary*. "I see things without understanding them. It took me ages to realize that what appeared to be splashes of blood all over the pavements of Bombay was merely people spitting betel juice" (78).

Finally, the brain's role in seeing explains another common phenomenon of travel: the fact that we tend to see all that is new and different in a foreign locale and apparently overlook everything that is familiar. It's not really that we overlook the familiar but only that the brain processes familiar sights so quickly that we recognize them almost at once, and we thus have the mistaken impression that we have not actually noticed them. Unfamiliar sights, on the other hand, stand out because the brain cannot immediately process them—something "doesn't look right"—and they attract and hold our attention for being initially unrecognizable.

Metaphorically Speaking

Before we conclude our brief survey of brain science, we might say a word or two about the language we have used thus far in this chapter. The brain is an enormously sophisticated, little-understood instrument; its inner workings are extremely complex, so much so that the kind of lay vocabulary appropriate for a book like this is not really up to the task of describing how the brain functions. Accordingly, the language we have used here—words like *input, memory bank, close matches, encoding, storing, retrieving*—is much closer to metaphor than to actual description; these words are meant to trigger images but they should not be interpreted literally. (Readers who are interested in the hard science—in knowing more about neurons, synapses, and glial cells—should follow up in some of the resources listed in the bibliography.)

That said, the broad outline of how the brain works presented here is consistent with the latest neuroscience; the brain receives impressions from the senses, processes those impressions, and then presents sights, sounds, etc. to us. But the details of that processing are where the complexity—hence, the metaphors—come in. Recent research suggests that the concept of a vast data bank or filing cabinet where the brain stores and then searches out memories may in fact be somewhat simplistic; it now appears that when the brain receives an impression from receptors, a synapse related to that impression "fires," which in effect leads the brain to the right visual memory. Be that as it may, if the metaphors here are somewhat crude, the big picture is sound.

The Greatest Gift

> Everything in the intellect has been in the senses.
>
> Thomas Aquinas

The preceding discussion of how the brain works helps us understand the significance of new experience, hence of travel. One of the most obvious conclusions we can make, staying with the sense of sight, is that each act of seeing informs and enhances all subsequent acts; the more we *have* seen, the more we are subsequently *able* to see. As you are exposed to and process new visual input, your visual memory bank grows, and the brain can draw upon this ever-expanding data base to inform your observations of all future scenes. Once you have seen and have visual memory of anything, an iceberg, for example, you will see that object the next time it appears in your visual field. In other words, we should remember that when we take in a particular scene, a landscape, let's say, we do not see what is in the landscape; we see what is in us. As we travel and have new experiences, thereby adding immeasurably to what is in us, we are able to see more and more of the world we live in. The more we see of the world the better we understand it. And the better we understand the world the better we can function therein.

Sense experiences are even more formidable when we consider the other role they play in our lives, and especially in the formation of the traveler: *sense experiences and the memory they create are the fundamental building blocks of all knowledge.* All knowledge begins with sense experience and can ultimately be traced back to experience. This is not to say that experience and knowledge are one and the same, for they are not, but only that knowledge is not possible without experience.

Nor do we mean that all knowledge comes *directly* from sense experience; a great deal of knowledge, most in fact, is derived from *other* knowledge, as the mind organizes and reorganizes the things it knows in infinite combinations, constantly adding what it learns from new experiences to the ever-changing mix. But even knowledge many times removed from sense experience, knowledge seemingly unrelated to its original source material—even this knowledge ultimately derives from our senses, however tenuous the link. Where else could knowledge come from?

The link between experience and knowledge is similar in many ways to the relationship between raw materials and manufactured goods. Raw materials are combined in myriad ways to produce all manner of finished products. And finished products are then combined with other finished products to produce still other, more refined products, each successive generation of product bearing less and less resemblance to the original raw materials. But none of these products, *however far removed they may be from their original source materials,* could exist without them.

There is an almost exact parallel of this sense experience-to-knowledge paradigm in the realm of language, specifically in the way concrete vocabulary (based on sense experience, the physical world) evolves into more abstract vocabulary (concepts and mental constructs). As Guy Deutscher points out in his book, *The Unfolding of Language*, almost any abstract word, including the word *abstract* itself, can be traced back to a concrete forebear with its roots in the physical world. "Why is it," Deutscher asks,

> that when one only scratches a bit, most abstract words turn out to have concrete origins? Why should the surge of metaphors always flow from concrete to abstract and so rarely in the other direction? Why do we say about legislation that it is "tough" but not about a steak that it is "severe"?
>
> The truth of the matter is that we simply have no choice but to use concrete-to-abstract metaphors. And when one stops to think about it, this is not even so surprising, since after all, *if not from the physical world, where else could terms for abstract concepts come from*? (127; italics added)

Deutscher asks readers to try an experiment wherein they choose the most "abstract of abstractions" they can think of and then trace it back to its origin. As long as "their pedigree is known," he writes, "chances are they will go back to some simple words from the physical world. The word 'abstract' itself is one such example, for what could be more abstract than that?... But the origins of 'abstract' are much more earthy, as 'abstract' comes from a Latin verb which simply meant 'draw away' (*abstrahere*)" (128).

And so it is with knowledge; even the most abstract, immaterial idea or concept—as completely removed from the physical world as it is possible to imagine—began with sense experience.

Let's consider an example of how knowledge derives from sense experience, one that gives us an excuse to quote a famous passage in one of the classics of modern travel literature: *Wind, Sand, and Stars* by Antoine de Saint-Exupery. Three Moors of

Saint-Exupery's acquaintance have been brought to France for their first visit outside North Africa, and while hiking in the Alps, they behold a waterfall for the first time.

> Some weeks earlier they had been taken up into the French Alps [where] their guide had led them to a tremendous waterfall, a sort of braided column roaring over the rocks.
>
> "Come, let us leave," their guide had said [after a while].
>
> "Leave us here a little longer."
>
> They had stood in silence...mute, solemn...gazing at the unfolding of a [great] mystery. The flow of a single second would have resuscitated whole caravans that, mad with thirst, had pressed on into the eternity of salt lakes and mirages. Here God was manifesting Himself. He had opened the locks and was displaying His puissance.
>
> "That is all there is to see. Come."
>
> "We must wait."
>
> "Wait for what?"
>
> "The end."
>
> They were awaiting the moment God would weary of his madness. They knew Him to be quick to repent, knew Him to be miserly.
>
> "But that water has been running for a thousand years". (104, 105)

Elsewhere, St. Exupery observed that "for the first time they realize the Sahara is a desert" (Schiff, 232).

This is practically a textbook example of sense experience morphing into knowledge. What actually happened here is that the Moors, with no experience (hence no sensory memory) of abundant water were exposed to a new phenomenon: a waterfall. They processed the experience and added it to their memory bank. When that happened, they suddenly had sensory memory of minimal or no water and sensory memory of abundant water, and when the two memories came together, the result was knowledge. The three Moors suddenly realized for the first time that they lived in a desert. As Frank Smith, our faithful guide to the mind in this chapter, has explained: "Comprehension may be regarded as relating what we attend to in the world around us to what we already have in our heads" (53).

Once we accept this fundamental link between experience and knowledge, then the profound significance of travel becomes self-evident. Why? Because ever since the Renaissance and the invention of the self, and continuing on up to the present time, mankind has considered the pursuit of knowledge—understanding ourselves and the world around us—as the noblest and most sublime of all human endeavors. And if knowledge ultimately derives from experience, then the significance of travel—the single greatest source of *new* experience—simply cannot be overstated.

It's not surprising that this notion of the link between knowledge and sense experience, hence between knowledge and travel, first came to be widely accepted in the 18th century when, as we saw earlier in this chapter, travel in the modern sense first began. From the 18th century onwards, the desire to accumulate experience and therefore expand knowledge has fueled countless voyages.

Paul Fussell has written that no one in the 18th century seriously questioned John Locke's argument that knowledge comes entirely through the external senses and from the mind's later contemplation of materials laid up in the memory as a result of sense experience. This meant...that what one knows results entirely from impingement on one's receptors of physical stimuli...Travel, therefore, became something like an obligation for the person conscientious about developing the mind and accumulating knowledge. *Observation* becomes virtually a duty, a*nd extensive observation* as well. (1987, 129, 130)

The fact that experience expands our knowledge is what observers for centuries have meant when they declared that travel profoundly changes the traveler. This is the central truth behind the countless tributes to the power and significance of travel, those grand statements that travel—take your pick—broadens your mind, expands your horizons, deepens your understanding, changes your perspective, alters your consciousness, adds to your personality. At the heart of all these sentiments is the same fundamental notion: the person who returns from the journey cannot possibly be the same person who set out.

All the great travelers and travel writers understood or at least intuited this truth, and many wrote about it. "True and sincere traveling is no pastime," Thoreau wrote, "but it is as serious as the grave, or any part of the human journey..." It is likewise what Robert Byron meant when he called travel "a spiritual necessity" and one of "the more serious forms of endeavor" (Fussell, 1980, 91).

Byron continued,

To travel in farther Asia is to discover a novelty previously unsuspected and unimaginable. It is not a question of probing this novelty, of analyzing its sociological, artistic, or religious origins, but of learning, simply, that it exists. Suddenly, in the opening of an eye, the potential world— the field of man and his environment—is doubly extended. The stimulus is inconceivable to those who have not experienced it. (Fussell, 1980, 92)

And the poet Goethe, in his *Italian Journey*, (27) gets right to the point. "Nothing," he writes, "is comparable to the new life that a reflective person experiences when he observes a new country. Though I am still always myself, I believe I have been changed to the very marrow of my bones." (27)

Old and New

Strictly speaking, *every* experience is a new experience, in the sense that it is not possible to have the same experience twice. We can experience the same external objects, the same stimuli, over and over again—the same set of buildings on our daily walk—but each encounter with those objects is a unique experience.

Nor is it the case that only new experiences add to our memory bank but that "old" ones somehow do not; *all* experience adds to our memory. The difference is a matter of degree; encountering the same sight over and over again adds subtle refinements to our visual memory, reinforcing and enhancing an existing memory, whereas seeing a new sight for the first time creates an entirely new memory.

The impact of familiar experiences is reassuring and calming; they reinforce and reconfirm what we already know. Unfamiliar experiences are unsettling and exciting; they expand our knowledge and often change what we thought we knew. Most of what happens to us at home confirms our assumptions and validates our instincts about the world. Much of what happens to us abroad challenges our assumptions and undermines our instincts. Abroad is not for the faint of heart nor for those who are attached to their views.

Finally, we should note that new experiences are not confined to travel, to being in new environments. By definition we have new experiences all the time, in entirely familiar environments as well as in unfamiliar ones. What is different about travel is the amount and variety of new experiences, unequalled in virtually any other human activity. "That is the thing about travel," Alec Waugh observes in *Hot Countries*. "It is not so much that one sees the world through it as that one comes to a whole new series of sensations that are to be won no [other way]" (288).

In this chapter we set forth a simple premise: that new experiences and what they lead to are the reasons travel matters. And now we can see why: if sense experiences do indeed create memory, and memory creates perceptions, and perceptions enable knowledge, then in due course new experiences—the very essence of travel—will enable new knowledge. And new knowledge leads inevitably to increased understanding, the noblest of all human pursuits.

If this seems like an inordinate burden to place on travel, a piling on of impossibly grand expectations, there is no need to worry, for as we will see clearly in the coming pages: travel does not disappoint.

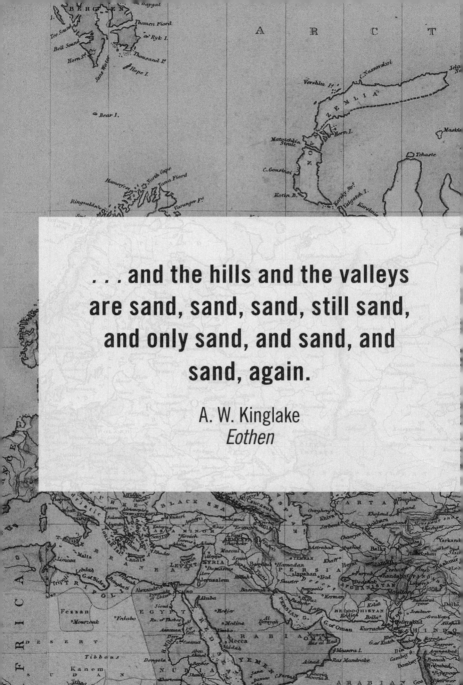

. . . and the hills and the valleys are sand, sand, sand, still sand, and only sand, and sand, and sand, again.

A. W. Kinglake
Eothen

CHAPTER 2

A New Place

In chapter 1 we identified the link between experience and knowledge, and we declared that travel, due to its high quotient of new experience, expands our knowledge of the world and ourselves more than any other human activity. In the next three chapters, we will take a closer look at the content of these new experiences, what we learn from them, and how that knowledge transforms us.

We can divide the experiences we have abroad and what we learn from them into two categories: what we learn through experiences of the place and through experiences of the people. The place includes everything *except* the people, and the people includes their behaviors, beliefs, values, and what lies behind all of these: the native mindset or worldview. Much of what we learn overseas comes through contact with the people, of course, but encounters with the place also change the traveler. Indeed, it's possible to have very limited contact with the people in a foreign locale and still be greatly transformed by the travel experience.

In some ways, the distinction between place and people is an artificial one, because we encounter them together—we interact with the people *in* the place—but we will separate them in these pages for ease of analysis. We will begin with a chapter on place because its impact is often overlooked and generally less understood.

We have combined the numerous dimensions of place into four somewhat arbitrary categories: the landscape, the climate, the structures or buildings, and everything else, or what have labeled "objects." In this chapter we will examine how our first-hand experience of these four phenomena adds to our knowledge and thereby enhances our understanding of ourselves and the world. We will explain, in short, how the experience of place begins to transform the traveler.

This transformation is an ongoing process rather than a series of neat steps, and while some of it is conscious, a great deal is unconscious. Moreover, while the process begins during the voyage, with direct observation and experience, the changes wrought by the place (and the people too, for that matter) evolve over time, much of them occurring long after the voyage has ended. The seeds of impact are planted during the trip through actual encounters with the foreign place. The insights and realizations that follow, however, while they *can* come during the voyage, are just as likely to emerge gradually upon reflection, and they are often triggered and enhanced by subsequent experiences back home that put the travel experience in perspective.

An Early Surprise

> After another mile or two, [Rome] appeared...in the distance; it looked like—I am half afraid to write the word—like LONDON!!! There it lay, under a thick

cloud, with innumerable towers, and steeples, and roofs of houses, rising up into the sky, and high above them all, one Dome. I swear, that keenly as I felt the ... absurdity of the comparison, it was so like London ....

Charles Dickens
Pictures from Italy

Contrary to all expectations, the first thing voyagers notice about abroad is that it doesn't look all that different from home. This will sound absurd to experienced travelers, not to mention disappointing to would-be travelers. Those old travel hands, after all, can regale you for hours with stories about the exotic, amazing, weird, and otherwise unbelievable things they witnessed overseas. And they're telling the truth; foreign locations *are* teeming with unusual, unfamiliar, and exotic phenomena, as we will see soon enough, but that's the *second* thing travelers notice about abroad, not the first.

So what do we mean when we say abroad doesn't look that different from home? To begin with we mean that while abroad does indeed abound in things that are new and unfamiliar, not *everything* about abroad is new and unfamiliar. There are many things abroad that we immediately recognize: buildings that look like buildings back home; chairs and tables just like those in our own dining room; cats, cars, and carrots in Cairo virtually identical to the cats, cars, and carrots we have back in Cleveland.

Another thing we mean is that even among those phenomena abroad that *are* unfamiliar, almost none of them are *completely* unfamiliar. There is almost nothing you will encounter in a foreign country that you do not have some version of back home, nothing so utterly unrecognizable that you can't even begin to guess what it is. So maybe you don't have minarets back home, but you may have church steeples; maybe you don't have pandanus, eucalyptus, or flame trees back home, but you do have trees. "What about camels?" you ask. "We don't have any camels back home." True, but chances are you have other four-legged animals. Granted: if you saw a three-legged, a five-legged—or better yet a no-legged—creature overseas, now *that* would be unfamiliar (although even then you would still know it was some kind of animal).

The traveler can be forgiven for not noticing the familiar when he goes abroad because that is almost literally what happens. If we recall the discussion (from chapter 1) about how the mind sees, we might remember that the mind processes familiar sights, anything it has visual memory of, almost immediately, so quickly that such sights make only the faintest of impressions on our consciousness, which is why we don't notice them. So it is with the traveler when he is exposed to familiar sights among all the unfamiliar sights in the foreign environment; while he doesn't exactly *over*look these sights, the looking happens so fast that the sights barely register. What register instead, of course, are all the unusual sights the traveler has never encountered before.

While travelers don't like to admit it and are typically not even aware of it, it's lucky so much about abroad resembles home, for if this were not the case, then most travel would not be possible. Think about it for a moment. What would it actually feel like if, during your first few minutes and hours overseas, you didn't recognize or understand anything around you, if *everything* you encountered was utterly foreign and unfamiliar? As a practical matter, you would be so rattled and stressed by this excess of novelty—so disoriented, overwhelmed, and threatened—that you would most likely panic and be unable to function. The presence of so much that is familiar, even if it barely registers, is sufficiently soothing to most travelers that they retain their faculties and continue their journey. The familiar, in short, creates the sense of feeling safe and in control, which ultimately enables the traveler to encounter the unfamiliar without becoming unhinged and jumping on the next plane home.

I had spent time in over 35 countries, many of them in the developing world, before I set foot in India for the first time. I had some cause to assume I had seen it all in terms of the novel and the unfamiliar, and initially, at the Delhi airport, my assumption seemed correct. There were some novelties, of course, but at any major international airport there are bound to be familiar sights and the feeling of security they offer. My next stop, however, was the Delhi train station, where the excess of novelty caught me completely off guard. The riot of colors, the many styles of dress, the varieties of headwear, entire families living in every unoccupied nook and cranny, separated by cardboard "walls," crippled beggars of every variety, the cows, the fruit sellers, the tea wallahs, the bangle sellers, the crushing throng of bodies, the smells, the howling din. I might have encountered some of these elements before but never altogether or in such intense profusion. I reeled initially, not exactly frightened but indisputably uneasy (I can still see the scene in my mind's eye even now), and then I slowly started picking out things I recognized and understood, and I began to believe I could cope. When the train pulled in, I was just calm enough to get on.

Landscape

In North Africa the earth becomes the less important part of the landscape because you find yourself constantly raising your eyes to look at the sky. In the arid landscape the sky is the final arbiter. When you have understood that, not intellectually but emotionally, you have understood why it is that the great trinity of monotheistic religions—Judaism, Christianity, and Islam—which removed the source of power from the earth itself to the spaces outside the earth, were evolved in desert regions.

Paul Bowles
*Their Heads Are Green
and Their Hands Are Blue*

One of the first differences travelers notice about going abroad is the landscape. If you're driving through Sinai, for example, on your way to St. Catherine's monastery, you are bombarded with all manner of new impressions: vast mountains of solid rock rising out of the desert, the near-complete absence of trees or any other vegetation, the sudden splashes of vibrant green beside a spring or hugging a riverbank, the occasional palm oasis, the unrelenting barrenness and dryness in every direction, the small herds of goats watched over by shepherd boys, the shattering brightness of the sun, the nearly complete absence of people, animals, water—and the hand of man.

Or let's say you're hiking in the foothills in Nepal, on your way to the Annapurna Sanctuary, and you round the last corner before entering the village of Ghandrung, clinging to the side of the mountain at 6,300 feet. Straight ahead, topping out at 24,688 feet, is the mountain known as Annapurna IV. You are struck by the amazing verticality of the landscape, the angular, jagged peaks, the bewildering array of tiny terraces, carving a field out of a hillside, by the massive bulk and incredible height of Annapurna IV, towering three and a half miles above you.

Travel begins in this manner, as an intense physical encounter with the unfamiliar, a veritable assault on the five senses and an enormous deposit in our sensory memory banks. It is an entirely visceral experience—we might call it raw travel—and it's thrilling, awe-inspiring, marvelous. This is travel as discovery, and it's one of the main reasons people want to leave home.

As the traveler is being overwhelmed by all manner of this new sensory input, something else is happening: he is forming impressions and reaching conclusions about the new landscape, making characterizations. It is arid and barren (in the case of our traveler in Sinai); the sun is shattering; the terrain is rocky. The peaks are jagged (in the Himalayas).

But here we must pause and ask a question: Why does this landscape evoke these particular impressions? Why does the traveler find the topography barren? Why is the sun so bright? Why does the terrain appear rocky? The answer, of course, is because the traveler has experienced *not*-barren, is used to a sun much less intense and to terrain covered in vegetation. To put this another way, it is almost certain that this same landscape would not appear barren or rocky to the indigenous shepherd boys, nor would the sun strike them as especially intense. Our traveler makes these particular characterizations because he is seeing Sinai (or the Himalayas) relative to his previous experience of landscapes. Judging from these specific impressions—arid, barren, rocky, and too bright—the traveler is used to geography that is not barren or rocky and where the sun does not shatter (or where the mountains are more modest). Let's say, then, that he comes from New England.

Obviously, then, even as the traveler is observing the foreign landscape passing by his car window, he is seeing in his mind's eye another landscape, which he contrasts with the one all around him and from the perspective of which he now describes Sinai. And what is this other landscape? Strictly speaking, it would have to be the encoded results of all previous experiences of landscape contained in the landscape "drawer" of the traveler's memory bank. But more simply put it would be the one with which the traveler has had the most experience, the one he has seen the most often and with which he is the most familiar—in other words, the landscape of home. It is because he comes from New England, then, that our traveler finds the Sinai barren; if he were from Jordan, say, or even from parts of the American southwest, Sinai would strike him quite differently.

It's important to recognize that all the comparing going on here is actually two-way: Even as the traveler conjures up New England in the act of characterizing and describing Sinai (albeit only in his mind's eye, for the moment), he is also taking in and encoding impressions of Sinai, impressions that are being deposited in the traveler's visual memory and will shortly be available to inform all of his subsequent observations, *including the way our traveler will now perceive New England when he returns.* In other words, just as it is because of New England that our traveler sees Sinai the way he does, it is likewise because of Sinai that he will eventually see New England in a new way, as stupendously forested, for example, shockingly green, its sun somewhat subdued and almost benign.

Now in his mind's eye and later in reality, the traveler will perceive aspects of his home landscape he has never noticed and will see familiar aspects from an entirely new perspective; in short, he will see more of home than he has ever been able to see before. Just as our Moors gazed upon an Alpine waterfall and understood for the first time they lived in a desert, our Yankee, confronted with Sinai, understands New England from an entirely new perspective. Thus it is that through encountering the exotic and the unfamiliar, the traveler's perception of home has been forever transformed.

The Figures in the Landscape

> Whether a landscape is bleak or beautiful, it doesn't mean anything to me until a person walks into it, and then what interests me is how the person behaves in that place.
>
> Mark Salzman
> *Iron and Silk*

But it is not merely the physical landscape of home that is so radically altered by travel. As the traveler takes in the foreign landscape, describing it with reference to his own and seeing his own from this new perspective, he can't help noticing the people going about their daily lives. In the example of Annapurna, the traveler might notice the village women in the foothills of Nepal walking three hours every morning down to the river and back, with huge jugs of water on their head. He realizes how carefully Nepalis must use water; he wonders who is looking after a woman's small children. (Her mother-in-law? An older daughter? Perhaps a niece?) He wonders what happens when the woman gets sick; maybe he wonders what the men do, about the division of labor in Nepali villages.

Or we can go back to the Sinai. As our traveler drives through the desert, he is going to be deeply struck by the towering rock outcrops, the barren, windswept, sweltering plateaus, the almost complete lack of human habitation; it is an austere, forbidding, utterly inhospitable landscape where the elements hold sway and man has barely a toehold. And it may occur to him (now or later in his voyage) that if he lived here, as some Bedouin do, he would not take his survival for granted. On the contrary, he would know with deep certainty that the only thing between him and utter ruin is a series of happy accidents: a handful of healthy goats, a she-camel that's still giving milk, and a rain squall that comes just in time. He survives in spite of his surroundings, not because of them. He survives because his luck hasn't run out.

These are not merely observations of landscape; they are observations of how people accommodate to and ultimately how they are shaped by their environment—observations of the profound impact of place on human behavior. And not just on the behavior of the locals, as significant as that surely is, *but also on the behavior of the traveler.* How? As the traveler witnesses the locals adjusting to their surroundings, beginning to sense how place has shaped the inhabitants of Sinai and Ghandrung, he must also begin to sense, even if only subconsciously, how the place he comes from—a place he now starts to see more clearly, thanks to travel—has shaped who *he* is. Any experience that sheds new light on our surroundings must inevitably teach us new things about ourself. How could our Moors who realize for the first time that they come from a desert not also begin to understand how their landscape has shaped their actions and even their ways of thinking? And how could they realize *that* and not understand themselves better?

The first time I went back home to Vermont after living in Nepal for a year, I was stunned by how puny and rounded the Green Mountains were and how effortlessly accessible, with roads running through them all up and down the state. They had never seemed small or accessible before, of course, but next to the Himalayas, giant barriers impossible to cross or even to skirt (without going 50 or 75 miles out of one's way), the Green Mountains were reduced to hills. No wonder I felt that the world was open, that I had a sense of possibilities, that my environment was pliant and manageable. All paths were open, even beckoning. Not so the mountain-dwelling Nepali, I reflected, whose world must feel dramatically closed, hemmed in beneath towering walls, for whom all paths stop at the base of impassable peaks. My world, I realized, gave me a sense of freedom. The Nepali's, I imagine, must inspire a deep sense of limits.

The Inner Journey

> Abroad, freed of the clutter and distractions of home, we see many things—especially our own people—more clearly and more tellingly than we would at home.
>
> W. Somerset Maugham
> *The Skeptical Romancer*

Travel, it turns out, is two trips in one: an outer journey that adds to our understanding of a foreign place and its people, and an inner journey that adds to our understanding of home and thus of self.

Travel is discovery, to be sure, but it is also *self*-discovery. "Journeys lead us not only outwards in space but inwards as well," Lawrence Durrell has observed. "Travel can be one of the most rewarding forms of introspection" (15).

The intrepid Swiss traveler Ella Maillart uses the word *relearning* to describe the consequences of seeing one's home from the new perspective of the foreign place. "Everything must be relearnt again," she observes as she heads off into the barren wastes of central Asia.

> Life can be truly gauged.... My way leads toward desolate lands, treeless and empty of habitations. I shall pass months in a solitude as old as the hills, but then I shall be able to judge what crowds mean to me. With all the weight of the heavens over my sleeping body, I shall know what a roof is. And cooking over a fire of dung, I shall learn the true worth of wood. (33)

Durrell, writing about the great English traveler and travel writer Freya Stark, notes that "a great traveler (in distinction to a merely good one) is a kind of introspective; as she covers the ground outwardly, so she advances towards fresh interpretations of herself inwardly" (Stark, 1988, Foreword).

The discovery of home and thus of self is one of the more profound consequences of travel. It is likewise one of the most important of those "mechanisms," as we called them in the prologue, that the express purpose of this book is to uncover and describe, those heretofore mysterious means by which travel guarantees that the person who returns from the journey is not the same one who set out.

Climate

> I've been in Ceylon a month and nearly sweated myself
> into a shadow.
>
> D. H. Lawrence
Letters

As with all things and people in the new place, the first thing we notice about climate in a foreign country is how different it is. Or, if it is not different, if it is similar to our home climate, then we will take no notice of climate at all. If we come from colder latitudes, we will feel the oppressive humidity of the tropics and marvel at the excess of rainfall. Or we will feel the aridity of the desert and the intense heat of the sun. If we come from the tropics, then we note the scarcity of rain in northern climes, the dryness of the air, the shocking novelty of snow and ice. Continuing our inner journey, meanwhile, we will see our own climate from this new perspective, understanding it in ways we never could before.

Next we observe the adaptations people make to their climate and how it shapes their behavior and lifestyle: the ways they cope with the humidity, with the overabundance of rain, with the absence of rain, with snow and ice, with the changes of the seasons. We imagine what it must be like during the three months of monsoon in Sri Lanka or three months without the sun in Scandinavia. And we begin to understand that climate, like landscape, is destiny. "No power of place," John Daniel writes, "is more elemental or influential than climate" (Espey, 367).

Richard Lewis has observed, how it is

> obvious that in such diverse countries as Finland, Russia,
> Chad, the Congo, Canada, Afghanistan, and Indonesia,
> climate will dominate, perhaps even define, customs, hab-
> its, viabilities, culture itself. Russia with its months-long
> frozen steppes, Finland with its long winter nights and its
> inhabitants' mighty heating bills, Saudi Arabia with its
> desert heat, and Singapore with its intense humidity are all
> [affected] by the severity of their weather. (17)

And Lewis goes on to give an example of the effects of climate,
explaining that how people greet and talk to each other is in part a

> direct effect of sunshine, heat and cold…Finns, Swedes,
> and Norwegians, meeting friends in the street in win-
> ter, indulge in only brief interaction, [with] the greet-
> ing…often compressed into a 20-second burst. [T]his
> culture of outdoor succinctness (called "winter behavior"
> by the Finns and the Swedes) carries over to their indoor
> communication habits, where economy of expression and
> the ability to summarize are prized.…
>
> [T]he influence of sunshine and heat on people's speech
> habits is [likewise] clearly discernible around the Mediter-
> ranean [where locals] spend a large part of their lives on
> the street…in roadside cafes, open-air taverns and res-
> taurants; on the waterfront; by the seashore; in the village
> square. In these locations conversation is not hurried, brief,
> or succinct.…Sunshine encourages outdoor dalliance, vol-
> uble discussion, unhurried examination of all aspects of a

question or issue. Much probing goes on, many avenues of persuasion are explored, fervent desires are pressed again and again. [While] the Nordic takes no for an answer and whisks herself off…the southern Latin…pleads, cajoles, demonstrates his wit, and entertains. (18–20)

In Morocco I once drove with some friends over the Middle Atlas mountains down to Zagora, "the gateway to the Sahara." After Zagora we continued on for another 90 kilometers towards Tagounit. The road became sand in many places, and along the way it rained for no more than two or three minutes, barely enough to have to turn on the windshield wipers. Soon after it rained, we picked up a teenage Moroccan boy and gave him a lift down the road to his village. "It rained a little," I observed. He looked confused: "It rained *a lot*," he said.

Just as with landscape, we experience and characterize the local climate—humid, dry, icy cold, oppressive, gloomy—from the perspective of our own, and then we see our own climate against the backdrop of the overseas locale, from an entirely new perspective. And then we notice how people adapt to their climate, how it affects their lifestyle, and we are prompted to reflect on how our own climate has influenced our lifestyle and how it explains in part many of our common behaviors and attitudes—how it has shaped our very self.

Buildings

For there are no immediately discernible laws of construction or decoration; each building seems to have a

fantastic prettiness of its own; nothing is exactly like
anything else, and all is bewilderingly novel.

Lafcadio Hearn
Writings from Japan

Another aspect of place that immediately captures the traveler's
notice is the buildings, the grand, ornamental ones and the common, everyday ones such as shops and homes. The traveler is
enchanted by minarets (or by church steeples), Hindu temples,
thatched cottages in the British Midlands, onion domes in Russia, Maasai huts in Kenya, kasbahs in the Sahara, 14th-century
wooden cottages in Hungary, the bazaar in Istanbul, the marketplace in Guatemala City, the large, wrap-around porches of homes
in Cleveland or Boston, by tiny, closet-size shops in the *souks* of the
Arab world, crammed with so much merchandise the owner has no
place to sit. Encountering these structures sheds light on how the
locals live and also brings the churches, homes, and marketplaces
of the traveler's home country into sharper focus, giving them new
meaning. "The architecture of a place reveals something about the
humanity that has flowed through it over the centuries," Eric Leed
observes, "for this architecture is the material residue...of all the
identities, behaviors, exchanges and meetings that make up [the
place]" (87).

This is especially true of homes, beginning with their general
appearance, their size, how close they are to each other, how many
windows they have and how big they are, what the houses are made
of, what kind of lot they sit on, and how the property looks. "Homes
are the most obvious expression of where a people come from," the
Indian author Pavan Varma observes. "[T]heir design is rooted in a

specific cultural milieu. And the needs they cater to profile a social context more vividly than most other things" (7).

In some countries, homes are surrounded by walls, sometimes with glass shards at the top. Many American homes have large picture windows looking onto the street, and some of the older ones have front porches facing the sidewalk, while in other countries there are few or no windows to the outside but a large open courtyard in the middle. In England, many homes have small front yards and spacious backyards, with beautiful gardens. In America, it is often just the reverse. In Tunis, most homes have a flat, open rooftop where you can sit in the sun and from which you can see halfway across the city. In urban areas of Europe, most people live in apartment buildings, creating vibrant city centers that come alive in the evening. In many American cities, people commute from the suburbs to the city center, which is reserved almost exclusively for commercial and office use and virtually empty after 6 p.m.

Merely by observing some of these features from afar, before there is any contact with the locals, the traveler begins to form all manner of ideas about what it must be like to live in these spaces, about what homes say about their inhabitants. How is an individual who grows up in a home with no exterior windows and a large interior courtyard different from another person who grows up in a home with big picture windows and a large front porch facing the sidewalk? Can these two possibly have the same values or the same outlook on life?

Frances Trollope, for one, seriously doubted it. Comparing 19th-century French plumbing to English plumbing, she notes that "great and manifold as are the evils entailed by the scarcity of water in the bedrooms and kitchens of Paris, there is another deficiency greater still: The want of drains and sewers is the great defect of all the cities in France, and a tremendous defect it is.... That people so circumstanced should have less refinement in their thoughts and words than ourselves, I hold to be natural and inevitable" (53).

The inside of people's homes is even more revealing about how they live: the size and arrangement of the various rooms, the furnishings, how the rooms are used. Until very recently, kitchens in the UK had very small refrigerators, no more than three feet high, necessitating almost daily food shopping. In Morocco, the guest only sees two rooms: the living room (where the guest also sleeps) and the bathroom; guests almost never go into the kitchen or any other room in the house (except for the roof).

"Americans revealed too much too soon about themselves," Richard Pells has observed, contrasting American and European homes:

> They seemed unaware of the pleasures of privacy or of secrecy. While Europeans [think] of their houses as castles or sanctuaries, surrounded by gates, hedges, or high walls... Americans [live] behind picture windows, their domestic arrangements 'exposed to the gaze of every passerby,' implying they [have] nothing to hide from the outside world. The Americans... [lack] the European talent for artful seductions and deceptions. (171)

On a similar note, Paul Theroux observed that it "was not just the quaint places in England that looked both pretty and inhospitable. Most villages and towns wore a pout of rejection—the shades drawn in what seemed an averted gaze—and there were few places

I went in England that did not seem, as I stared, to be whispering at me all the while, *Move on! Go home!*" (Theroux, 2006, 20).

How do Japanese homes, with small multiuse rooms and sliding, removable walls made of paper, shape the people who grow up in them? "[M]ost 'western homes' clearly distinguish between a living room, a dining room, and a bedroom," John Condon has written.

> In the traditional Japanese home, however, a single room can serve all three of these functions, and thus it is sometimes difficult to speak of the bedroom or the dining room, for it may depend more on the hour of the day than the areas themselves....Moreover, the doors which separate most rooms are also lightweight sliding doors which can be removed entirely when necessary....These sliding doors have no locks. One cannot go into his own room and lock the door.
>
> This aspect of home structure seems consistent with contrasting values of Japanese and Western peoples. That is, the family as a whole, rather than the individual, is highly valued in Japan. As the action of any one member of the family reflects on the entire family, individual choices and decisions must be made with great care and after considerable discussion within the family. (155, 156)

We hasten to add that travelers won't suddenly understand all this merely from observing the inside of a Japanese home. But if they do get invited to one, they can't help noticing how a Japanese home differs from their own home, and they might reflect on what these differences must mean for life lived in such a place.

Greg Nees draws similar cultural conclusions about Germans and Americans by contrasting certain differences in how their homes are arranged and how guests are treated.

> The open architecture typical of American houses and apartments in which the front door opens into the living room is not common [in Germany]. Walk into a traditional German home or apartment and you will usually find yourself in a small, closed corridor, or *Gang*. This corridor provides access to the other rooms of the house or apartment, and the doors to these other rooms will generally be closed (2000, 48).
>
> Similarly for guests invited into a German home, there are clear boundaries to be observed. Giving guests a "tour of the house," as often occurs in American homes, is rare in Germany. Americans often do this to show off their house and to create a relaxed, informal atmosphere so that their guests feel at home. Dinner guests in Germany rarely get to see the inside of the kitchen, let alone a tour that includes the bedrooms. Germans maintain a formal atmosphere by having the house perfectly neat and orderly.... (47)

Just *who* the inhabitants are in a typical home is also a window into the culture. In the West, single- or nuclear-family homes are the norm, but in India the sons traditionally brought their brides to live in their parents' home, with enormous consequences for the daughter-in-law/mother-in-law relationship. In many cultures, other relatives and several generations may live in the home, such as elderly parents, never-married siblings, widowed aunts and uncles, cousins going to school or looking for a job in the city. "I cannot remember a time, growing up in India," Shashi Tharoor writes, "when there wasn't a young man from either of my parents villages in Kerala—sometimes not even a close relation—living in our flat while my father arranged for him to have some professional training and get him a job" (289).

Growing up in such a home—surrounded by cousins, grand-parents, nieces, in-laws—is a fundamentally different life from growing up in a nuclear family, and it produces fundamentally different people. And you don't have to meet or talk to a single one of these people to sense that they must be very different from you; it's enough just to see their home.

While you can in fact learn a lot from a distance, as noted above, it's true that the grand prize is somehow to get an invitation to someone's home. Accordingly, we will address that challenge at some length and offer several suggestions in chapter 5: How to Travel.

Office buildings and especially workplaces likewise reveal a lot about the locals. When you enter an office building and observe how the offices are laid out, their size, how they are furnished, and generally how the space is used, you begin to form impressions about work life and values. In America, for example, managers often get the famous corner office, somewhat apart from the staff and always with a door and at least one window, while junior staff often work in more open spaces such as cubicles with little or no privacy. In many American workplaces an office or a cubicle near a window is highly prized and a perk for more senior staff. In Japan, by contrast, the manager often sits in the center of one or more con-centric circles of subordinates, with senior staff closer in and junior staff and new hires in the outer rings. In this configuration, staff by the window are typically either the most junior or people close to retirement. Indeed, the term "window people" refers to employees in Japan who are quite literally no longer at the center of things and nearing the end of their career.

How people in offices use their doors offers another insight into culture. "[D]oors remain closed in most German...office buildings," Nees observes,

> where a closed door does not mean a private meeting is taking place but only that the door is closed as Germans notions of orderliness and clear boundaries dictate. This is a noticeable contrast with the open-door policy of many American businesses....Germans say they keep their doors closed so they can get their work done. After all, they argue, you go to work to work; if you want to socialize, go to the movies. (48, 49)

Travelers typically don't spend a lot of time in office buildings, of course, except for business travelers. But any time you go into a bank, for example, or a post office, or even just your hotel, you may get a glimpse now and then of people in their work spaces and impressions of work life.

With buildings, as with climate and landscape, the inner and outer journeys unfold together. Even as the traveler contrasts local buildings with those at home, noticing numerous differences, he is also getting new impressions of the buildings he grew up with, seeing them from the perspective of a Japanese home, for example, or a Middle Eastern marketplace. Seeing many things about these buildings for the first time, especially about how they reveal and/or influence the way people grow up, the traveler is bound to understand new things about himself.

Objects

> A plug socket, a bathroom tap, a jam jar or an airport
> sign may tell us more than its designers intended; it
> may speak of the nation that made it.
>
> Alain de Botton
The Art of Travel

Abroad is full of stuff, and stuff makes impressions. This category—
objects—is something of a catchall; it includes everything in a foreign locale that is *not* the people, the landscapes, the climate, or
the buildings. Cars are objects, for example, as are Arab *dhows*,
oxcarts, and rickshas. Roads are objects, and canals, trails, and
footbridges. Fauna are objects: dogs, camels, toucans, rhinos, and
llamas. All the things inside a house, an office building, or a temple
are objects. Everything in the market is an object.

The impact of objects can be initially overwhelming, an explo-
sion of new sense impressions, as the Englishman Charles Kingsley
observed on his visit to Trinidad in 1869. "[I am] actually settled in
a West Indian country house," he writes,

> amid a multitude of sights and sounds, so utterly new and
> strange that the mind is stupefied by the continual effort to
> take in or, to confess, to gorge, without hope of digestion,
> [impressions] of every conceivable variety. The whole day
> long new objects and their new names have jostled each
> other in the brain.... Amid such a confusion, to describe
> this place as a whole is as yet impossible. (84)

Gradually, individual objects emerge from the blur and the
traveler takes note. The impact of objects on the traveler is similar

to the other categories described above: he encounters the object; he marvels at it if it is something he has never seen before (his first giraffe) or if it is an especially unusual version of something he has seen before (a very old car, a very shaky footbridge); he notices how the object is used by the locals; and he sees his own objects and how they affect him from this new vantage point.

Walking through the bazaar in Tunis you will come across an entire section devoted only to olives and another just to dates, and when you leave the bazaar you will know something about Tunisians you did not know before. When you're trekking in the Himalayas and pass a man carrying a refrigerator on his back, you intuit something about what life is like in a place with no roads. As you continue down the trail and come to a footbridge that has been washed away, you are bound to wonder what that means for the people living in the area. When you see a lion in the Serengeti lounging near a Maasai village, you wonder what it's like to have predators for neighbors and the risk of taking a pee outside at two o'clock in the morning.

As distinct from landscape, climate, or buildings, the impact of encountering new objects seems to be more subtle, perhaps because there is such a profusion. As such the reflections it triggers about the local lifestyle and, hence, about one's own, come more slowly. But they are no less eye-opening than those we have attributed to the other elements of place. Let's use roads as an example. Some years ago if you took the main road from Nairobi to the Maasai Mara game park in central Kenya, you.... Well, that's just the point: you could *not* take the road because it was so poorly maintained as to be impassable. The asphalt was broken up and the roadbed itself was full of holes, some of them big enough to swallow a small car. Folks still made the trip to Maasai; they just didn't go on the road. Instead, they bounced along on a rough track parallel to the road.

The traveler on such a journey could not help but compare this road to the roads back home and intuit all manner of notions about how inefficient transport must be in Kenya, how that must effect the availability and price of goods along the road, how the condition of the roads might affect response time in a medical emergency, and endless other speculations. Or imagine what goes through the mind of the traveler trekking to villages in rural parts of the Himalayas where there are no roads, only narrow trails. Encountering the objects of place teaches the traveler a great deal about how people live and about how the traveler himself lives. Would our traveler from New England ever see his own roads the same way or take them for granted after that trip in Kenya?

Paul Bowles captures perfectly the subtle influence of objects on individual behavior in his description of how the absence of cars in the medina (the old city) of Fez, Morocco, affects the inhabitants. "Fez is still [such] a relatively relaxed city," he writes,

> there is time for everything...in part at least [because of] the absence of motor vehicles in the Medina. If you live in a city where you never have to run in order to catch something, or jump to avoid being hit by it, you have preserved a natural physical dignity that is [missing] in contemporary life; and if you still have that dignity, you want to go on having it. So you see to it that you have time to do whatever you want to do; it is vulgar to hurry. (2010, 451)

The Impact of Place

> One's destination is never a place but a new way of see-
> ing things.
>
> Henry Miller

It's been a busy day for our traveler, and we might pause here to make sense of all that has happened. We need to continue constructing our answer to the question at the heart of this book: How does travel change the traveler? In the present instance, how has the encounter with a new place altered the observer? Or, as Somerset Maugham would have it: What has the traveler added to his personality?

Whatever lessons the traveler learns from the place he visits will be in almost direct proportion to how different that place is from his home. If Germans go to Austria or Egyptians go over the border to Libya, they will be in relatively familiar surroundings and will not, therefore, be exposed to quite so many entirely new phenomena. In our analysis here, we are assuming the traveler has visited a place that is both physically and culturally quite different from his home.

At the subconscious level, the traveler has made an enormous deposit in his sensory memory bank, receiving and storing innumerable new sense impressions, with all the advantages described in chapter 1. Going forward the traveler will see more of the world around him, will see familiar things from new angles and more fully, and will bask in the benefits that follow whenever sense experience magically evolves into knowledge and understanding. If human beings truly *are* the sum of their experiences, then the traveler has added immeasurably to himself.

At another level, the traveler has observed firsthand how the four elements of a place influence its inhabitants. If people are shaped by their place, then different places will shape their inhabitants very differently. But those inhabitants, however different they may be from the traveler, behave just as normally and act just as logically in their place as the traveler does in his. It is one of the greatest lessons of travel: the discovery of the many varieties of normal.

At this stage, this realization is more of a feeling or an intuition than a fully formed thought, but it will grow and mature as the traveler begins to interact with the people (our subject in chapter 3) and encounter whole new ways of thinking (chapter 4). Yet even at this early stage, as the traveler does little more than take in impressions of the new place and casually observe the behavior of the locals from afar, he may begin to sense some mildly disturbing doubts about the universality of his own behavior. We will return to this theme in the next chapter.

As we've already seen, another result of the traveler's encounter with the foreign place is the discovery of his own place. As he confronts the foreign surroundings, he characterizes and makes sense of them relative to his home surroundings. Thus the traveler begins to see many aspects of his home landscape, climate, buildings, and objects in completely new ways, adding greatly to his understanding of his place of origin. Arthur Young, writing of a trip to France in 1787, explained how his journey confirmed for him "the idea that to know our own country well, we must first see something of others. Nations figure by comparison" (Black, 324). We would add that if individuals are shaped by their place of origin, which the traveler has now begun to understand in ways he never could before, then any added understanding of one's home translates automatically into a greater understanding of oneself.

In Nepal there is only one real word for road—*baato*—which means "trail." There is another, made-up word, which translates into something like car-going *baato,* but basically there's just *baato.* And for a very good reason: until recently there was nothing *but* trails in most of Nepal, especially in the hill country. This got me to thinking about all the terms we have for roads in America: *street, road, dirt road, highway, divided highway, turnpike, interstate.* That in turn made me realize how easy it is to go anywhere in the states. As a result most Americans have a real sense of how different the different parts of our country are and, therefore, of how things that might apply or be true in one part would not be true in others. I know how we live different lives in different parts of the country; I know that many people are not like me. I have encountered difference. But a rural Nepali, I would imagine, whose trails cannot take him very far, has probably not; he must believe that most places are the same and most people are just like him.

It might be stating the obvious to point out one additional effect of travel: the successful encounter with so much that is foreign and unfamiliar, the experience of surviving such an unprecedented onslaught of novelty, changes forever the traveler's attitude toward what is different. Difference is no longer disturbing or somehow unsettling, something to be feared. The traveler has been improved by difference, his sensitivity has been enhanced by difference, his understanding deepened. After their first taste of difference, most travelers, not surprisingly, can't wait to taste it again.

The same goes for our attitude toward the unknown, another beast slain by travel. Almost by definition, what is unknown is somehow forbidding; it stirs apprehension, makes us anxious, and is even vaguely threatening. But once we have traveled and confronted the unknown, it loses its power over us. When early

European mapmakers drew the Atlantic Basin, they marked all the places explorers had discovered, but in the empty spaces beyond, where no one had yet ventured, they simply wrote *Here be dragons*. When we travel and meet the dragons, the world becomes a much less unsettling place.

These, then, are among the earliest effects of travel on the personal development of the traveler. More effects are still to come, and these same effects will only intensify as the traveler starts to spend time with the locals. But even if the journey ended here, with nothing but experiences of the foreign place, the traveler could still be assured of coming home with a very different self from the one with which he started out.

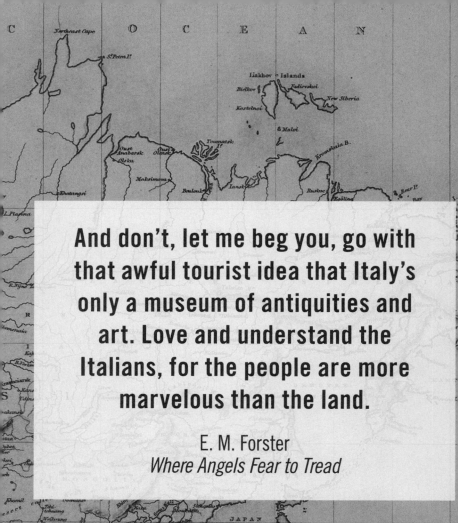

And don't, let me beg you, go with that awful tourist idea that Italy's only a museum of antiquities and art. Love and understand the Italians, for the people are more marvelous than the land.

E. M. Forster
Where Angels Fear to Tread

CHAPTER 3

New People

If, as Alexander Pope so pithily observed, the proper study of mankind is man, it follows that any self-respecting traveler should, by rights, be more interested in the natives of the country in which he travels than the country itself.

John Julius Norwich
A Taste for Travel

Much of what travelers learn from their encounter with the place is not immediately apparent, not something the typical traveler is necessarily aware of or could consciously articulate. Yet the process of comparing and characterizing has unmistakably begun, as well as the process of seeing home and oneself in completely new ways. The encounter with place, however, and the lessons it begins to reveal are to some extent dwarfed by those that come from contact with the people, which is our topic in this and the following chapter.

It's quite possible to travel without having any significant contact with the locals and still be changed by the experience, by the encounter with place alone. But this would not be very satisfying to the serious traveler. It's easy to see why: while encountering an unfamiliar place certainly begins to transform the traveler in ways we have described, encountering the people deepens and completes the transformation. Those things travelers can only guess about foreigners from being in their physical surroundings can be confirmed and greatly expanded upon by getting to know the people. Moreover, whatever brief glimpses and insights into one's home and self the traveler gains from encountering a new place, encountering the people opens up a veritable panorama of self-discovery. If the impact of place on the traveler is significant, the impact of people borders on the profound.

"I assume it is natural for a traveler to seek diversity," Paul Bowles writes,

> and that it is the human element which makes him most aware of difference. If people and their manner of living were alike everywhere, there would not be much point in [travel]. With few exceptions, landscape alone is of insufficient interest to warrant the effort it takes to see it. Even the works of man, unless they are being used in his daily living...take on the qualities of decoration. What makes Istanbul worthwhile to the outsider is not the presence of the mosques and the covered souks, but the fact that they still function as such. If the people of India did not have their remarkable...spiritual discipline, it would be an overwhelmingly depressing country to visit, notwithstanding its architectural wonders. (1984, vii)

Not That Different

> Thus you see, dear sister, the manners of mankind do not differ so widely as our voyage writers would make us believe. Perhaps it would be more entertaining to add a few surprising customs of my own invention; but nothing seems to me so agreeable as truth....
>
> Lady Mary Wortley Montagu
> *Letters*

We will go out and meet some locals in just a moment, but before we do we need to examine two unexpected insights travelers have early on about the people, realizations that seem to contradict everything travelers think they know about travel. The first is the realization that foreigners are really not all that different from the folks back home, similar to the discovery described in chapter 2 that many things about foreign places look quite familiar. This sounds absurd, of course, since we all know that foreigners are very different from us—that's why we call them foreigners—and that's why we travel: to meet people unlike us and broaden our minds in the process. Indeed, the less they are like us, the more exciting we find them. Travel books and returning travelers are full of wonderful anecdotes about the peculiar, amazing, and in some cases shocking ways foreigners think and behave.

All true, of course, but the stubborn fact remains that among the very first things travelers notice about the locals are impressions of sameness. Actually, "notice" is demonstrably not the right word here, for these impressions of sameness are not conscious, not something travelers observe or are aware of. Rather, they are completely subconscious, something travelers instinctively intuit or sense, something they immediately apprehend but nothing they would be able to describe. While it is differences of place and people that *strike* travelers and command their attention, the similarities make almost no impression, slipping in largely unnoticed.

So it is that as surprised and fascinated as travelers are by the strange appearance and unusual behavior of foreigners, they are simultaneously comforted and reassured by all manner of recognizable appearances and shared behaviors. You won't hear much about these similarities when travelers return—they're subconscious, as noted, and they also don't make for very good stories—but they are no less real or less important. Indeed, if it were not for the conviction deep in the traveler's psyche that the locals are essentially like the traveler, then travel as we know it would not be possible.

Why? Because if *everything* about the locals in a given foreign location were utterly different from everything about us—if we had no idea how they were going to react to or behave toward us—travel would be a very iffy proposition. If you could not be sure, for example, that the locals would not hunt you, cook you, make you their pet, or otherwise seriously inconvenience you, would you be quite so keen to go overseas? If the locals were aliens, in other words, and not merely foreigners, would you feel quite so secure in their midst? Indeed, doesn't the tension in science fiction novels and films stem precisely from the fact that no one knows for sure just how the aliens are going to behave? Would you really go to Mars without a weapon?

And yet we *do* feel secure in the midst of most foreigners in most locations, and that is precisely because we recognize their essential humanity, that they are *fundamentally* like us even if there are some exotic, perplexing, and even annoying differences. The simple fact is that we instinctively recognize and understand much of what the locals are doing overseas—their behavior is not completely novel or entirely random—and as a consequence we feel comfortable and safe among them. The locals are variations on a theme, in other words, but they are not an entirely new theme. If you're even moderately relaxed and calm the first night in Mexico or Madagascar, it must be because to some extent you feel at home. A lot of things do change when you travel—and quite a few stay the same. Just as this was true for the place, it's also true for the people.

But Why Am I So Surprised?

> It produced a curious feeling, almost fear, this first contact with persons, clothes, and observances of utter strangeness. For many years I had thought about Tibet, read about it, and gazed longingly at photographs of its huge landscape and fantastic uniforms. None the less, the reality came as a shock.
>
> Robert Byron
> *First Russia, Then Tibet*

The second, even more surprising realization we travelers have early on is that apparently we're expecting the locals to be just like us. Another absurdity, the reader is thinking. We *know* they're not like us; that's why we want to go abroad in the first place. Is there a serious traveler anywhere who would not be deeply disappointed to discover that foreigners are just like her?

Probably not, but that doesn't change the facts.

Consider this: If we *were* actually expecting foreigners to be different from us, then how do we explain the inconvenient fact that most of us have very strong reactions to foreigners and all the odd things they do? Travel books, not to mention returned travelers, are full of stories about the surprising, frustrating, amusing, shocking, and annoying ways the locals behave. But if we really do know that foreigners are not like us—if we really *are* expecting them to be different—then why are we so surprised when that's exactly how they turn out? If they're not like us, they *should* be different.

This odd riddle at the heart of the travel experience is not quite as illogical as it first sounds. In fact, we do expect travelers to be different from us *in a general way*; we just have no idea precisely what those differences are going to be, in what *ways* foreigners are going to think and act differently from us. While we can expect *difference*, in other words, we cannot anticipate *specific* differences. Simply put, we cannot expect something we have never experienced.

Back home in our own culture, surrounded by people more or less like us, we have years of experience of people thinking and behaving in certain ways. These consistent, endlessly repeated patterns (called "norms") become deeply engrained in our subconscious and develop into our instincts, automatic ways of thinking and acting, the basis of what we call normal—and the reason, incidentally, that we are able to function in our own culture: because everyone else has the same instincts. This accumulated life experience of normal constitutes our culture's version of reality.

And there's the rub, for while this is actually only *our culture's* version of reality, most of us, if we have not experienced any other version, naturally assume that this is everyone's reality. It's *the* truth, in short, not just our truth. And that is why we expect foreigners to be just like us, because up until the time we actually meet a foreigner, everybody always has been.

But surely we know better, you're thinking. We read books and watch documentaries; we have friends and relatives who've been to the Amazon and the Sahara. It's not like we live in a cave. True enough; you do *know* better. But what you are up against here is the relative strength of logic versus experience, the mind versus the senses. When these two clash, it's not a fair fight. What we know secondhand through indirect, occasional exposure to a foreign reality (movies, books, friends' stories) can never compete with what we know firsthand, through direct and regular exposure to our everyday reality. We may have heard about other versions of reality, but we have not been surrounded by, immersed in, and continually bombarded by them.

And that makes all the difference. When logic squares off against experience, experience always wins. So while logic may tell us that foreigners will be different, the weight of our experience tells us they will be just like us. "Like most people who have never traveled abroad," the novelist Sinclair Lewis writes of his title character in *Dodsworth*, "Sam had not emotionally believed that these 'foreign scenes' veritably existed, that human beings really could live in environments so different from the front yards of Zenith suburbs, that Europe was anything save a fetching myth" (69).

So it is that you can sit in your living room, sipping tea, reading how some French people actually take their dogs to restaurants and still be shocked months later, dining out in Paris, when you glance over and see Fifi, propped up on a Louis XIV chair, eating quietly out of her master's hand.

"There is all the difference in the world," Aldous Huxley has written,

> between believing academically, with the intellect, and believing personally, intimately, with the whole living self. A deaf man who has read a book about music might

be convinced, theoretically, that Mozart was a good com-
poser. But cure his deafness [and] take him to listen to the
G Minor Symphony; his conviction of Mozart's greatness
would become something altogether new. (1985, 207)

Elsewhere Huxley ties this notion to the experience of travel.
"Of the fact that it takes all sorts to make a world," he writes,

I have been aware ever since I could read. But proverbs are
always platitudes until you have experienced the truth of
them. The newly arrested thief knows that honesty is the
best policy with an intensity of conviction which the rest
of us can never experience. And to realize that it takes all
sorts to make a world one must have seen a certain number of the sorts with one's own eyes. (1985, 207)

Our friend Antoine de Saint-Exupery was more succinct:
"Truth is not that which can be demonstrated by the aid of logic,"
he wrote. "Let logic wangle its own explanation of life" (187).

Logic, the intellect, the facts, the mind—call it what you will—
they all tell us that foreigners are going to be different. But until we
actually encounter the locals, we will never be true believers.

Appearances

> Our tight clothes appear to them not
> only ridiculous but indecent.
>
> R. R. Madden
> *Passionate Pilgrims*

In the previous chapter, we saw how encountering the place begins to transform the traveler; now it's time to look at the effects of encountering the people. There are two ways a traveler is affected by meeting the locals: by observing their behavior and by becoming aware of their mindset or worldview, that which lies behind and produces their behavior. In this chapter our topic is behavior, including appearances; we will consider the impact of different worldviews in the next chapter.

Appearance is in fact the first thing travelers notice about the locals, specifically their physical features and how they dress. It all depends on where you go, of course, and especially on how different the place you travel to is from your home. If you travel to a country culturally and racially similar to your own, if an American goes to Holland or an Indian goes to Sri Lanka, neither the physical features nor the dress of the locals will be that different from back home, and you may not even notice them. But if you go to a place that is culturally and racially very different, if an American goes to Kenya or a Kenyan goes to Chicago, then differences in appearance are immediately apparent.

Let's start with physical features. The Caucasian North American who goes to China or to sub-Saharan Africa doesn't look like the Asians or Africans all around her, and very few of them look like her. For first-time travelers and for those who have not been to a racially different destination before, this will be a brand new and possibly unsettling experience: to look very different from almost everyone else in their surroundings, to stand out and be immediately noticed, to look abnormal, even odd. In a word, to look precisely like what you are: a foreigner. It's ironic that we travel to encounter difference, and yet one of the first things that happens to us overseas is to discover that *we are the ones* who are different.

As we are busy noting the unfamiliar physical features of the locals, we can't help but notice that in many cases the locals don't dress like us either. The first time you go to Tunisia, you're going to see women in veils and a lot of men in *djellabas* (a kind of V-neck shirt that keeps going all the way down to the ankles). If you visit the Punjab, ancestral home of the Sikhs, you'll see men wearing a turban and *kurta* (a long, loose shirt) and women wearing *salwar* (loose-fitting pajama-like pants) and *kameez* (like a *kurta*). If you go to central Kenya, you'll see Maasai women wearing the *kanga* (a kind of shawl) and men wearing the *shuka* (a traditional blanket). All over India you'll see women in saris and men in *loongis* or sarongs.

This probably won't be the first time the traveler has encountered people who are dressed differently—most of us have seen foreigners wearing their national dress in our own country—but what distinguishes this experience is that so *many* people are dressed this way. This style of dress is not an individual aberration or the affectation of a handful of nonconformists; it's how people dress in this place.

For most travelers, this observation of a different style of dress is their first significant encounter with difference (with respect to the people, that is). This is not like observing how the locals have unusual facial features or a different skin color. For all the traveler knows, people with a different physical appearance might still think or act the way the traveler does; this is not conclusive proof of difference. But when the traveler bumps into men wearing a *kurta* and a turban, she instinctively knows these cannot be like people who wear Levis and a Yankees' cap. She does not know how the locals are different from her just yet, but there can no longer be any doubt of the fact that they are different. The traveler has had her first experience of the foreignness of foreigners.

It was just such an experience that inspired one of the great passages in travel writing in one of the acknowledged 19th-century classics of the genre: *Eothen* by A. W. Kinglake. A British traveler to the Middle East in the 1830s, Kinglake describes his first encounter with real difference, riding through the countryside outside Constantinople: "But presently there issued from the postern [city gate], a group of human beings—beings with immortal souls, and possibly some reasoning faculties, but to me the grand point was this, that they had real, substantial, and incontrovertible turbans" (3).

Kinglake is exactly right; these individuals may indeed have immortal souls and some reasoning faculties—in other words, they may indeed be like him in some respects—but the whole point is they're wearing turbans. And not just any turbans, but *"real, substantial, and incontrovertible"* turbans (italics added). These are turbans, in short, that cannot be gainsaid or denied, and these are people, therefore, who cannot possibly be like him.

Nor is it only the unusual clothing that prompts this realization in the traveler, but also what is covered and what is not covered by clothing in a particular country. In some Muslim countries, every inch of a woman's body is covered, including the face, while men's faces are not covered, except perhaps by a beard. In western countries, a woman's breasts are always covered, but not in some traditional African tribes. The sari leaves a woman's midriff bare. As travelers make observations like these, they are beginning to sense other differences about the locals: that they probably have different concepts of modesty, different notions of what is erotic, different attitudes toward male-female relations, different views of gender.

With dress, then, the discovery of real difference has begun; the traveler now knows she is in the presence of people not like herself. What's more the traveler may even have a vague notion of the nature of some of the differences between herself and the locals (even as she has similar notions from observing the foreign place), but she will not be aware of the depth nor the variety of differences until she actually begins to interact with the locals, until she encounters their behavior.

First Contact

> Everyman calls barbarous that which he is not accustomed to.
>
> Michel de Montaigne

After the traveler checks into her room and takes a shower, she goes out to have a coffee—and with any luck, she won't ever be quite the same again. Barring a scene at the airport or some drama with the taxi driver, this is the moment the traveler is no longer just observing difference but actually experiencing it through direct contact with foreigners.

As travelers sip their coffee, they will of course see many things they recognize and understand, but they will begin to see numerous behaviors they have never witnessed before and do not understand. It is in these observations of unfamiliar behavior, of people saying and doing things the traveler would never say and do in comparable circumstances, that travelers finally come face to face with, as Kinglake might put it, real, substantial, and incontrovertible proof that the locals are not like them. It's the moment of truth for serious travel.

We will examine presently how these first-hand encounters with difference transform the traveler, but all this will be easier to understand if we consider some examples. One hardly knows where to begin, as the categories, to say nothing of the individual instances, of cultural differences among people, are legion. Or as the 18th-century English traveler Tobias Smollett has colorfully put it:

> There is nothing so vile or repugnant to nature but you may plead prescription for it in the customs of some nation or other. A Parisian likes mortified flesh; a native of Legiboli will not taste his fish until it is quite putrefied; the civilized inhabitants of Kamschatka get drunk with the urine of their guests, whom they have already intoxicated; the Nova Zemblans make merry on train oil; the Greenlanders eat in the same dish as their dogs; the Caffres, at the Cape of Good Hope, piss upon those whom they delight to honor and feast upon a sheep's intestines, with their contents as the greatest dainty that can be presented. (55)

Name a human activity or specify a set of circumstances, and it's a fair bet that somewhere some group exists that performs that act or behaves in those circumstances very differently from you and me. How people eat, what they eat; how they bathe; how they drive; how they worship, who they worship, and where they worship; how they treat waiters, teachers, parents, strangers, bosses, subordinates, clients, those younger and those older; how siblings interact; how people form friendships, how the sexes interact, how they date, how they wed, and who chooses whom they wed; how married couples interact, how they manage their household, and how they raise their children; how people conduct business, negotiate, run meetings; how people behave in all manner of settings such as shops, the office, other people's homes, cafes and restaurants, classrooms, the post office, bank, barber shop, grocery store, and gas station; how much they trust each other, who they trust, how they express approval, disapproval, joy, anger, embarrassment, and the whole range of human emotions. And there are innumerable differences in all the categories of nonverbal behavior: eye contact, gestures, facial expressions (more than 500 have been isolated), personal space, body postures, touching, queuing, and beckoning, to name just a few.

The list is exhaustive, and these are just the categories of difference the traveler may encounter; within each category, of course, there are innumerable examples of behaviors that vary greatly from culture to culture. The traveler will become aware of differences in behavior in two ways: she will remark on the odd ways the locals behave, and she will become aware of how oddly she behaves in the eyes of the locals. She will be dazzled by the strangeness of foreigners even as she dazzles by her own strangeness, with life-changing consequences.

How They Are Not Like Us

> We admire what we recognize and guffaw like a donkey at anything that would not happen in the cosy familiar whirl of Deal and Bournemouth and Blackpool.
>
> Hugh and Pauline Massingham
> *The Englishman Abroad*

We travelers all have our own tales, but travel writing is surely the richest source of stories about the foreignness of foreigners, so we

have elected to sample some of the classics of the genre to present
our catalogue of some of the ways foreigners are not like us.

Charles Doughty, the famous explorer of what he called Arabia
Deserta, got upset when his Bedouin companions chided him for
eating pork, and he chided them back:

> I see you eat crows and kites, and the lesser carrion eagle.
> Some of you eat owls; some eat serpents. The great lizard
> you all eat.... Many eat the hedgehog; in some villages
> they eat rats. You cannot deny it! You eat the wolf, too, and
> the fox, and the foul hyena. In a word, there is nothing so
> vile that some of you will not eat it.
>
> Charles Doughty
> *Arabia Deserta*

And where Doughty went, many have followed:

> I am not the type, monsieur, who feels himself superior to
> the rest of humanity. Indeed, I am no better than others.
> But these people, these Afghans. They are not human. "But
> why do you say that?" You don't see why, monsieur? Have
> you eyes? Look at those men over there. Are they not eat-
> ing with their hands? With their hands! It is frightful.
>
> Robert Byron
> *The Road to Oxiana*

It amuses me to notice the way the Indians reverse the
order in which we do things. For instance, at home men
take off their hats when they come into a house; Indians
keep on their turbans, but take off their shoes. We beckon

with the palms of our hands turned inwards; they beckon with them turned out. My ayah lays my slippers in a row with the toes pointing towards me. The cook begins to read his Hindustani book of recipes from the last page backwards, and writes his accounts from left to right, and *saws inwards*, which makes one nervous! And when they play cards, they deal from the undermost card in the pack, and send them around by their right. They think it rude to laugh, but they never hesitate to yawn.

Lady Anne Wilson
Letters from India

I was once called in to advise [a multinational] firm that has operations all over the world. One of the first questions they asked was, "How do you get Germans to keep their doors open?" Closed doors gave [my clients] the feeling that there was a conspiratorial air about the place and that they were being left out.

Edward Hall
Understanding Cultural Differences

In America they said "How do you do" and walked on by; and before I had time to answer, the person who had spoken was ten paces behind me, so that my reply, when it finally came, encountered the chest of the next man I met.... What kind of question is that to put to anybody? *How do you do*? Throwing a meaningless question like that in my face in the middle of the street....

Knut Hamsun
Selected Letters

In this arrangement of the day no circumstance is so objectionable as that of dining at noon...for as the ceremony of dressing is kept up, you must be home from any morning's excursion by twelve o'clock....Dividing the day exactly in halves destroys it for any expedition, business, or enquiry that demands seven or eight hours' attention....I am induced to make this observation because the noon dinners are customary all over France. They cannot be treated with too much ridicule or severity for they are hostile to every view of science, to every spirited exertion, and to every useful pursuit in life.

Arthur Young
Travels in France

Indians do seem uncouth to the European. I shared the compartment with fat Mr. Jain, a vegetarian with swollen lips of the kind known as "sensual," mouth and teeth red-stained from betel juice, who punctuated the dark hours with snores and farts and hawkings—all Indians appear to do this. Yesterday morning an American family was having breakfast with their guide who, in mid-conversation, gave vent to an elaborate hawking and clearing of the passages; they regarded their cornflakes expressionlessly.

James Farrell
Indian Diary

There are *two* Italies. The one is the most sublime and lovely contemplation that can be conceived by the imagination of man; the other is the most degrading, disgusting,

and odious. What do you think? Young women of rank
actually eat—you will never guess what—garlick!

Percy Bysshe Shelley
Letters

Each car we passed raised a cheer from my fellow passengers. I closed my eyes as, tires screeching, we took a blind
corner, swerving across into the right-hand lane. This too
raised a cheer. Did death mean nothing to them? They had
slipped beyond my imaginative reach. The driver, wedged
between the angle of the door and the seat, could hardly be
bothered to glance at the road ahead. Frequently he would
remove both his hands from the steering wheel, the better
to emphasize some point to the fat lady sitting next to him,
with whom he was deep in conversation. Out of the corner
of my eye I caught a fleeting glimpse of a chicken plum-
meting past the window. A terrific commotion ensued. We
stopped, and a search party was organized. The chicken
was found alive, but stunned, and restored to its place on
the roof rack.

Shiva Naipaul
North of South

Once, from behind a closed door, I heard an English-
woman exclaim with real pleasure, "They are funny, the
Yanks!" And I crept away and laughed to think an English person was saying such a thing. And I thought: They
wallpaper their ceilings! They put little knitted bobble
hats on their soft-boiled eggs to keep them warm! They

don't give you bags in supermarkets! They say sorry when you step on their toes! Their government makes them get a hundred-dollar license every year for watching television! They charge you for matches when you buy cigarettes! They live in Barking and Dorking and Shellow Bowells! They have amazing names, like Mr. Eatwell and Lady Inkpen and Major Twaddle and Miss Tosh! And they think *we're* funny?

Paul Theroux
The Kingdom by the Sea

The [Senegalese] men walked hand-in-hand, laughing sleepily together under blinding vertical glare. Sometimes they put their arms round each other's necks; they seemed to like to touch each other, as if it made them feel good to know the other man was there. Two of them went about the whole day without loosing hold. It wasn't love; it didn't mean anything we could understand.

Graham Greene
Journey Without Maps

All over the world one can make oneself understood by gestures. But in India, impossible. You make a sign that you are in a hurry, that one must be quick, you wave an arm in a manner that the whole world understands, the whole world, but not the Hindu. He does not take it in. He is not even sure it is a gesture.

Henri Michaux
A Barbarian in Asia

Then [the old man] came around to the front of the truck to speak to the driver, who, being a good Moslem, wanted to get a shower and wash himself.... [He] was a city Moslem as well as being a good one, so that he was impatient with the measured cadence of his countryman's speech and suddenly slammed the door, unaware that the old man's hand was in the way.

Calmly, the old man opened the door with his other hand. The tip of his middle finger dangled by a bit of skin. He looked at it an instant, then quietly scooped up a handful of that ubiquitous dust, put the two parts of the finger together and poured the dust over it, saying softly, "Thanks be to Allah." With that, the expression on his face never having changed, he picked up his bundle and staff and walked away. I stood looking after him, full of wonder, and reflecting upon the difference between his behavior and what mine would have been under the same circumstances. To show no outward sign of pain is unusual enough, but to express no resentment against the person who has hurt you seems very strange, and to give thanks to God at such a moment is the strangest touch of all.

Paul Bowles
Their Heads Are Green and Their Hands Are Blue

Horace Walpole sums it all up quite succinctly in his remarks about the differences between the English and the French: "What strikes me the most upon the whole is the total difference of manners between them and us, from the greatest object to the least. There is not the smallest similitude in the twenty-four hours. It is obvious in every trifle" (Walpole, 102). And that's France, just across the channel. What would Walpole have thought if he'd gone further afield, to Constantinople, say, or Damascus?

How We Are Not Like Them

> The ideal traveler is...a man who goes out to learn. He is a person who...even as he wickedly observes the Italians juggling with spaghetti or listens to the tiresome yodeling of the Swiss, can look at himself and realize that he is equally funny.
>
> Hugh and Pauline Massingham
> *The Englishman Abroad*

And now some examples of the other experience of difference, wherein it is the traveler who behaves oddly in the eyes of the locals:

> I was travelling with a few of the nobles by train. Seeing 'Beef' on the menu, I ordered it. The waiter said Beef was off, so I had something else. Later, back in Dewas, the Maharajah said to me, with great gentleness, "Morgan, I want to speak to you on a very serious subject indeed. When you were travelling with my people you asked to eat something, the name of which I cannot even mention. If the waiter had brought it, they would all have had to leave the table. So they spoke to him behind your back and told him to tell you that it was not there. They did this because they knew you did not intend anything wrong, and because they love you.
>
> E. M. Forster
> *The Hill of Devi*

Washing my face in the morning caused much speculation at the village of Las Minas; a superior tradesman closely cross-questioned me about so singular a practice.

Charles Darwin
The Voyage of the Beagle

[The women of the harem] pitied us European women heartily, that we had to go about traveling and appearing in the streets without being properly taken care of—that is, watched. They think us strangely neglected in being left so free, and boast of [how closely they are watched] as a token of the value in which they are held.

Harriet Martineau
Eastern Life

My first shock came when I was requested, politely but firmly, by the guest-master to remove a pair of underpants then fluttering happily from the line. This, he pointed out, was a monastery; shirts, socks, handkerchiefs might be dried with propriety...But underpants were a shameful abomination...[B]ut worse was to come. I woke the following morning at dawn...and made quietly for the wash-house, covering myself from head to foot in a deep and luxurious lather. At this point the guest-master appeared. Never have I seen anyone so angry. I was now compounding the [earlier] sacrilege by standing stark naked under the very roof of the Grand Lavra. I was the whore of Babylon, I was Sodom and Gomorrah, I was a minion of Satan. I was to put on my scabrous clothes at once and return with all speed to the foul pit whence I had come.

Robert Byron
Mount Athos

But our English trick of shaking hands, they look upon as the most hoity toity impudent custom in the world and cannot reconcile it with the vestal demeanor of the English Ladies.

Catherine Wilmot
An Irish Peer on the Continent, 1801–03

The first mosquitoes of the year appeared at Nomo Khantara and as I killed one on my arm the lama sadly reproved me. To show me how to act in such circumstances, he took a sand-louse that was marching on to my rug and, handling it gently, deposited it outside the tent.

Ella Maillart
Forbidden Journey

Also that a Russian invariably takes off his hat whenever he enters beneath a roof, be it palace, cottage, or hovel; the reason for which is that in every apartment of every Russian house there hangs in one corner of it, just below the ceiling, a picture of the Virgin. To omit conforming to this usage and paying respect to the [gods] of the dwelling will not be either wise or well-bred, for it may give offense.

John Murray
Handbook for Northern Europe

A little golden girl of seven...brought in a coconut which she had opened under the tree outside, sat down, and offered it to me cupped in both hands, at arm's length, with her head a little bowed. "You shall be blessed," she murmured as I took it. I did say, "Thank you" in reply, but even after that I should have returned her blessing word for word, and after that I should have returned the nut also, for her to take the first sip of courtesy; and at last— when I received it back, I should have said "Blessings and Peace" before beginning to drink the milk. All I did—woe is me!—was to take it, swig it off, hand it back one-handed, empty, with another careless, "Thank you."

"Alas," she said at last in a shocked whisper, "Alas! Is that the manners of a young chief of [the white people]?" She told me one by one the sins I have confessed...but that was not the full tale. My final discourtesy had been the crudest of all. In handing back the empty nut, I had omitted to belch aloud. "How could I know when you did not belch...that my food was sweet to you? See, this is how you should have done it!" She held the nut towards me with both hands, her earnest eyes fixed on mine, and gave vent to a belch so resonant that it seemed to shake her elfin form from stem to stern. "That," she finished, "is our idea of good manners," and wept for the pity of it.

Arthur Grimble
A Pattern of Islands

We might add, for the record, that in addition to travel writing, there is actually a second entire genre of books, those dealing with international business and social etiquette, which likewise set forth an enormous panoply of cultural differences. These volumes meticulously describe all the dos, donts, and taboos that foreign visitors must be careful not to run afoul of. The section headings of these volumes, usually covering a large number of countries, suggest the myriad surprises awaiting the uninformed: dress, greetings, leave-taking, names/titles/forms of address, gift giving, dining out, guest etiquette, table manners, tipping, driving, taxi etiquette, meeting manners, giving presentations, humor, conversation style, taboo topics, and punctuality.

The world is full of the unfamiliar, the unexpected, and the extraordinary. Travelers react in various ways to all these differences; they are in awe of some of them and alarmed by others; they heartily approve of some and are thoroughly disgusted by others; they are offended by some and delighted by others; they are by turns shocked, surprised, amused, frustrated, annoyed, and fascinated. But they are never unmoved.

The New Normal

> Take it easy darling, he would say. We've got to be absorbed into these customs. We're still too tough to be ingested quickly, but we've got to try and soften ourselves. We've got to yield.
>
> Anthony Burgess
> *The Enemy in the Blanket*

Our examples have shown us what differences in behavior look like, some of the many forms they take. Now it's time to consider *what it means* to encounter these differences, how they affect the serious traveler and, ultimately, how they change her. It all begins with the shock of observing otherwise sane people, people who appear to be normal in many other ways, suddenly acting very odd. And not just one or two individuals, mind you, but so far as one can tell an entire population. In other words, this is apparently "how these people are," not just how a few oddballs behave.

When we are confronted with very convincing evidence that an entire group of people all behave in ways we have heretofore considered abnormal, we are obliged to accept the fact that such behavior is not abnormal at all. On the contrary, judging from all the evidence available to us, said behavior is manifestly and indisputably normal. And our own behavior, moreover, may not be nearly as normal as we think.

To understand better how this works, let's follow a single example of an encounter with difference and note carefully where it takes us. We'll use an often-cited difference between Europeans and Americans: the fact that the former don't usually acknowledge people they meet casually—on the elevator, say, or in passing on the street, such as on the way to the subway or bus stop, or while out walking the dog. In many parts of Europe unless you have been introduced to someone, you don't know them, and if you don't know them, you have no business greeting them. In many instances, Europeans would not even make eye contact or smile in such situations. For their part, Americans would certainly smile under these circumstances, many would also nod and say hello, and not a few might venture something like, "Nice day, isn't it?" All well within the American cultural mainstream—and quite unusual for many Europeans.

Two American expats told me very similar stories about this phenomenon. In the first story a woman living in Poland recalled how she was walking through a narrow alley one day, too narrow for two people to pass, when she noticed an elderly Polish lady approaching from the other end. The American knew enough to know she should squeeze up against the wall and let the elderly lady pass first. But when the lady was just opposite her, the American made eye contact, smiled, and said hello. Whereupon the Polish lady launched into a veritable harangue, berating the American for acting as if these two knew each other. "Do I know you? Of course I don't. Have we been introduced? Never. Do I greet and talk to strangers? Not bloody likely" (or the Polish equivalent). And some other choice observations about how rude it is to impose oneself on complete strangers.

The other story was about an American family living in a residential neighborhood in Frankfurt. The father used to walk the family dog every morning before going to work, and he often met the wife of the German family from across the street who was out walking her dog. He always nodded and said, "Good morning," and she always looked straight ahead and said nothing. "We also waved whenever we pulled out of our driveway," he said. He actually knew these behaviors annoyed Germans, he said, "but I just couldn't help myself."

This story has a classic last act: after two years in the neighborhood, the Americans were posted to England. On the day the moving van was parked out front, being loaded with their household belongings, the German lady came running over, very distraught.

"What are you doing?"

"We're moving to England."

"But you can't move! We don't know you yet."

Many American travelers in Europe would initially find this behavior off-putting and unfriendly and even be inclined to label

Europeans "rude." But then travelers, if they had their antennae out, would begin to notice something curious: it's not just the occasional European who behaves that way but most Europeans. So now the traveler must confront the fact that either most Europeans are rude or there is some other explanation for what's going on. At the edge of the traveler's consciousness, a nagging feeling begins to take hold that something's not quite right.

The matter might end there if the incidence of unusual behaviors remained low, but in fact it's quite likely—indeed, it's virtually inevitable—that the traveler will encounter a whole string of such incidents in no time at all, situations, that is, where whole groups of locals are behaving very differently from the traveler and yet the same as each other. In other words, the traveler will experience multiple instances wherein everybody's behaving very oddly *and yet nobody notices*—nobody but the traveler.

Against this barrage of evidence, it becomes increasingly difficult for the traveler to hold onto the idea that it's the locals who are unfriendly, strange, odd—choose your word. If most people behave a certain way *and it does not provoke a reaction*, then by definition that behavior must be normal. The traveler may not know why it's normal and may never find out, but of the fact that it is normal there can be no doubt.

Varieties of Normal

If you have lived about, you have lost that sense of the absoluteness and sanctity of the habits of your fellow patriots which once made you so happy in the midst of them.... You have seen that there are a great many *patriae* in the world and that each is filled with excellent people for whom the local idiosyncrasies are the only thing that is not rather barbarous.

Henry James
The Art of Travel

This is the moment serious travel comes into its own, the moment the traveler is confronted with undisputed proof of the reality of difference. If an entire nationality accepts as normal what the traveler regards as odd and surprising, and if those same nationals find the traveler's behavior demonstrably abnormal, then clearly the traveler's concept of "normal" is in urgent need of revision. What the traveler now begins to understand is that there are varieties of normal and that her particular version is just one of many. She sees, in short, that much of what she had always thought of as universal, as human nature, is cultural and thus only natural for some humans.

As the traveler becomes aware of culture and realizes that "normal" is something of a moving target, she begins to intuit that she cannot possibly see the locals the way they see themselves. After all, if she finds local behavior odd, confusing, and illogical, and if the locals regard the same behavior as perfectly normal, then clearly that behavior means something very different to the locals than it does to the traveler.

At this point the traveler realizes one of the great truths about human behavior: that it has no inherent, built-in meaning, no meaning that attaches to the behavior itself. Behavior means whatever people decide it means, or, in the case of a foreign culture, whatever everyone in that culture *agrees* that it means. Needless to say in many cases people from different cultures will assign a different meaning to the same behavior. We just saw this in the example

of the American and the Polish lady; Europeans assign one meaning to greeting strangers—that it's intrusive and imposing—and
Americans assign another meaning: that it's being warm and open.

Whenever two cultures assign different meanings to the same
behavior, then there's a very good chance that when a person from
one culture (our traveler) encounters people from another, she will
interpret local behavior from her own point of view. And she will
frequently be wrong.

As the traveler interacts more and more with the locals, coming across all manner of puzzling or annoying behaviors that
clearly do not puzzle or annoy the natives, she begins to realize
how often she must be misinterpreting them, how easy it is to be
mistaken about them (e.g., Europeans are rude), and how unwise it
is, going forward, to trust her judgments of the locals. She doesn't
know the nature of her mistakes yet, doesn't understand why her
interpretations are often incorrect—and may never even find out—
but she knows she has to be wrong about the locals. Either that
or she is forced to conclude that in European culture everyone is
rude *and no one minds.* Such a person will always be a force for
good in society because she knows how dangerous it is to judge—
and especially how dangerous it is to *act*—before understanding.
Aldous Huxley cautions us that we should always "try to understand before we condemn" (1985, 19). It is one of life's great lessons,
and nothing teaches it as well as travel.

This realization that we don't see other people the way they see
themselves, that we frequently misjudge them, is half of a two-part
discovery; the second half is that other people don't see us the way
we see ourselves. Even as our traveler is busy interpreting local
behavior from her culture's point of view, she begins to realize that
surely the locals must be interpreting her behavior from theirs.

She understands that even as she regularly misinterprets and misjudges the locals, they are no doubt regularly returning the favor.

The realization that we do not see ourselves the way others see us is just as important as its corollary, since it places the many misunderstandings we must endure in life in an entirely different and more positive light. How so? Because if you assume that other people understand you—that they see things the way you do—then when it becomes apparent they do not, it's only natural to conclude that such people are foolish, illogical, or simply ignorant. And you are consequently disturbed, unsettled, perhaps even vaguely threatened by their lack of understanding. But what if you were aware that people sometimes assign a different meaning to your behavior from the one you intended? Then you would realize that when they misunderstand you, it's not because such people are illogical and ignorant—no more than you are, anyway—but that they simply act according to a different logic and possess another kind of knowledge. While it can be disturbing and unsettling to live among the ignorant and the foolish, it's another matter altogether to live among those who are merely different. The world is a much kinder place, in short, when you understand that most people most of the time aren't trying to upset you.

There is yet another benefit to be gained from encountering the odd behavior of the local people, one we touched on briefly in the last chapter: such encounters make the traveler feel more at home in the world. By its very nature, difference makes us uncomfortable; it's only human, after all, to be wary, suspicious, even intimidated by what we are not used to and do not understand. But as we travel and encounter the unusual and the unexpected at every turn, we begin to grow accustomed to and develop a new attitude toward difference; we become less threatened by it and more open to it.

(Or we're overwhelmed by it and beat a hasty retreat.) The more we are exposed to difference—the more experience we have of surviving contact with people and situations we do not understand—the more at ease we are in the world around us.

Our traveler has had a very busy day, filled with insights or at least the raw materials thereof, and she is not the same person who woke up that morning. She has encountered difference on an unprecedented scale, her reaction to difference, as a result, has been necessarily tempered, and the way lies open to her eventual acceptance of the other. Robert Macfarlane, an English traveler to a place called the Basin on the Isle of Skye, remarked that observing life as it was lived "in the Basin, even briefly, is to be reminded of the narrow limits of human perception, of the provisionality of your assumptions about the world" (Fleming, 281).

This discovery of the limited and provisional nature of what we think of as normal is a direct attack on ethnocentrism, on that abiding belief in the rightness of our views and the absolute truth of our experience. It's simply not possible to realize that behavior we consider utterly strange is completely banal in a different culture and still maintain the same confidence in our experience. We must either accept that our reality, our truth, is relative or believe that everyone not from our culture is abnormal.

The profound significance of this effect of travel cannot be overstated, for ethnocentrism, after all, is the breeding ground of intolerance and the ultimate origin of all conflict. How can any experiences that undermine ethnocentrism and diminish intolerance, even in just one person, not be a positive good for the world? If travel accomplished nothing else, this result alone would guarantee its place on the list of life's most profound pursuits.

"[O]n a personal level," Vikram Seth writes, "to learn about another great culture is to enrich one's life, to understand one's own country better, to feel more at home in the world, and *indirectly to add to that reservoir of individual goodwill* that may, generations from now, temper the cynical use of national power" (italics added, 177, 178).

These remarkable changes do not happen all at once; the traveler does not wake up the second morning in Kenya suddenly grasping the meaning of culture and realizing she should suspend her judgments and not react. But the elements for such changes are all in place, and the process that will lead to them has been set in motion. So long as the traveler gets up every day and goes out to encounter the strange world around her, so long, that is, as the traveler continues to accumulate experiences of difference, she can look forward to the time when she will see the world and herself in whole new ways.

But the work of the true traveler is not quite finished. From observing the behavior of the locals, the traveler grasps that they must think differently, that they must have a different mindset, but that does not mean she knows how they think or understands their mindset. Observation by itself only teaches the traveler that the locals *must be* different; to understand what those differences are and to be changed by that understanding, the traveler has to engage with the locals. "As it is with the [rain] forest," Charles Kingsley, writes, "so it is with the minds of the natives. Unless you live among the natives, you never get to know them. If you do this you gradually get a light into the true state of their mind-forest" (xvii).

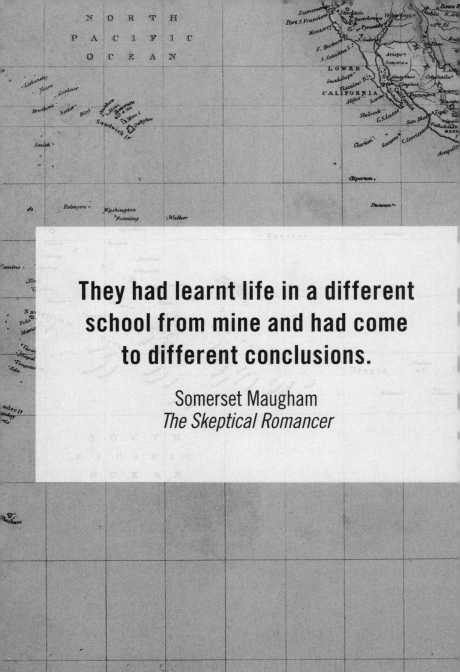

They had learnt life in a different school from mine and had come to different conclusions.

Somerset Maugham
The Skeptical Romancer

CHAPTER 4

A New World

> One thing I have always believed, and that is that one really learns nothing from a foreign country unless one...does something that really involves one with the inhabitants.
>
> George Orwell
> *A Life in Letters*

Our traveler could go home at this point, without interacting in any significant way with the locals, and still hold his head high, still be assured of bringing back a very different self from the one he set out with. After all, he has come to accept that there are many varieties of normal and logical, that some of what he thought of as truths are only views, and that differences need not be threatening. He readily accepts that the sometimes odd and incomprehensible behavior of foreigners must somehow be completely legitimate, although he could not tell you why. The traveler realizes he does not really understand the locals, but he knows he could. Should he decide to linger, a whole new world awaits him.

Observing behavior, then, has alerted our traveler to the likelihood of an entirely different worldview in the mind of the locals, but until now the traveler has not gained access to that worldview. While the behavior of the natives does indeed *reflect* what they are thinking, it is the thoughts themselves that matter. In this chapter the traveler will take the last step on his journey to self-improvement: he will come to understand an alien mindset—the Holy Grail of all serious travel.

Looking for a Mindset

> Every country has its own way of saying things. The important point is that which lies *behind* people's words.
>
> Freya Stark
> *The Journey 's Echo*

But how can we be so sure there's a mindset or worldview lurking behind people's actions? How do we know that if we go looking for the reasons why people behave the way they do, we will find something? Isn't most behavior spontaneous and automatic? Do people really stop and think before they act? Isn't behavior something we learn from our parents and elders and then copy? Why must it be the case, in short, that people who behave differently must therefore think differently?

Excellent questions. Behavior *is* spontaneous and impulsive in many cases; many behaviors *are* automatic and subconscious; most behavior is indeed learned. And no, by and large, people *do not* stop and think about what they are doing. None of which changes the facts. Even if people do act automatically, without thinking, even if they are not consciously aware of why they're behaving the way they do—even if they could not explain their behavior to someone else—it is never accidental and it always makes sense.

But if behavior is not random or accidental, then where does it come from? How is it that we already know how people are going to behave most of the time and thus feel safe leaving our house every morning? Behavior is ultimately the visible result of a series of deeply internalized, unchanging values and beliefs. These values in turn determine what is right and wrong, good and bad in any given society—patterns of behavior usually referred to as *norms*—thereby regulating how people behave and defining what that society regards as normal for a variety of common interactions. These values and beliefs are the reasons why behavior makes "sense" to the people of any given culture, and they comprise what we have called *mindset* or *worldview*.

A Worldview in Action

> The other guests left this morning, and just before starting Mrs. Montgomery gave me final advice: "You'll never understand the dark and tortuous minds of the natives," she said, "and if you do I shan't like you—you won't be healthy."
>
> J. R. Ackerley
> *Hindoo Holiday*

For an example of the link between mindset and behavior—of a mindset *in action*—we might return to our story from chapter 3

about the different ways Europeans and Americans regard strangers. In general, the northern European mindset values privacy
more highly than association, the natural instinct being to not
impose oneself on others rather than to connect with them (which is
the American instinct). Hence, the Polish lady who finds it rude when
an American she has never met greets her as they squeeze past each
other in a narrow alley. This doesn't mean Europeans do not value
associating with others, but rather that such association should occur
only under certain circumstances. The key difference with Americans, as we will discuss later, is that there are far fewer—indeed,
almost no—circumstances under which Americans would consider
it inappropriate to greet and otherwise interact with strangers.

Cultural experts have put forth a number of explanations for
the European sensibility or mindset vis a vis strangers. A common
one points to the continent's history of war and disease to account
for the relative wariness and even distrust with which many Europeans instinctively react to people they don't know. From earliest
times until the 20th century, in Europe the stranger represented
danger; someone outside his valley or district might carry the
Black Death, or he was a bandit, or an outcast (for God knew what
crimes), or a soldier in an enemy army come to pillage, rape, and
murder, or even a member of a friendly army low on rations, living
off the land—*your* land, that is. Stuart Miller cites a study of eleven
European countries over 2500 years, which found that "from one
century to another . . . one year in five is a year of armed conflict.
War is a normal condition" (8).

Elsewhere Miller has observed that

only by plunging ourselves into a sense of the enormous
weight of historic violence can we begin to understand the

European soul. We must think of a vast South Bronx of a continent, repeatedly devastated not for ten or twenty years but, as men experience time, forever.... The background of collective violence, combined with other historical forces like memories of massive poverty, makes the European closed and defended in ways that are typically un-American. (17)

Small wonder that in a world where the outsider represented danger and risk, the habit of reaching out never caught on.

Another explanation for the seemingly closed European exterior cites the remaining vestiges of the class system. In many Europeans countries, one did not commonly or comfortably interact with people outside one's social class, and when the classes did interact—when the valet dressed the lord of the manor in the morning, when the upstairs maid served tea in the library—they behaved according to certain time-honored scripts that regulated nearly all aspects of the interaction, thereby preventing as far as possible any awkward lapses in decorum. The valet might see the lord in his underwear (though almost never vice versa), but he and his lord were not friends and certainly not confidants, nor did they aspire to be.

This keen sensitivity to class, to one's station in life, inevitably carried over into being careful not to associate with those outside one's station, whether above or below; it was just too awkward *for both parties*. As wealth and opportunity proliferated and it became increasingly difficult to assess class, the natural instinct for many was to err on the side of caution (i.e., not connecting) when it came to strangers. Once one was introduced, of course, that changed everything. One would have to be introduced by someone who knew both parties, and such an individual could naturally be counted on not to make the mistake of trying to impose an individual from one social class upon an individual from another.

"I've clocked introductions by Americans in public places," Polly Platt writes.

> It's almost instantaneous, [after] about five seconds. [But] you can wait until the cows come home in France. This isn't rudeness; it's another marvel of politeness *a la Francaise*. For [the French], it's indiscreet to introduce people at an accidental encounter. One of them might not wish to be known to the other. (245)

Apart from the value Europeans place on privacy, another reason they're not in any hurry to connect is the almost total absence of urgency. Europeans identify with their village or their region much more closely than do Americans; by and large they are not a mobile people (though this is changing with the advent of the European union, especially for younger people). One is born, grows up, marries, and raises a family all in the same village or local area. And so do one's children. The temptation to move would have to be very strong, certainly stronger than the prospect of a better-paying job or even career advancement, to overcome the advantages of staying put, such as the ties to family and extended family and the sense of security that comes with living in one's homeland. As Miller has written, "A past in which, for more than two thousand years, social and economic movement were utterly exceptional" prevents the average European "from seeing himself or others as going anywhere" (154).

The contrast with the United States could hardly be greater: more than 40 million Americans, almost one-eighth of the population, change their address *every year*. Thirty-eight percent live outside the state they were born in, and approximately half the population of the major American cities changes every decade. "Many [European] visitors were impressed with how readily Americans moved from one place to another," Richard Pells has written,

> how prevalent their assumption that they could improve their luck by changing their address or embarking on a new career. To Europeans who normally went to school, married, and spent their adult years living in the same house and working at the same job, all within a few miles from where they were born, America appeared to be a nation of nomads. (170)

If you're not going anywhere, if you're going to spend most of your life in the same 20-mile radius, sooner or later you're going to meet almost everyone. Where's the rush to impose yourself on people you don't know? In due time, you'll be properly introduced.

For Europeans, in short, there has to be a reason to associate or connect with others, and in the absence of any reason, association would feel extremely awkward, even embarrassing. For Americans, proximity alone is a reason; it's sufficient for two people to occupy the same space at the same time for them to interact. Or, to put it another way, Americans don't need a reason.

Let's give the French the last word: "It's only by chance that we live so close to each other," the French writer Raymonde Carroll says of the other tenants in her apartment building,

> and this is not a sufficient reason for us to develop a relationship, unless of course, we specifically choose to do so. Similarly, on a small, quiet, provincial street it suffices for

me to nod my head and to say hello to the neighbors who
live next door and across the street (unless an extraordinary event interrupts the routine).

   In the absence of any relationship, silence is [normal]....
This is why in the elevator, in the street, on the bus, and
in practically every place where the other is almost totally
foreign to my daily life, where the context does not call for
ties to be formed, people don't talk to each other (27).

As these explanations demonstrate, European behavior vis a
vis strangers makes perfect sense once it's clear where Europeans
are coming from. And it is just that kind of clarity, about all manner of local behaviors, the traveler can look forward to once he has
engaged with the locals and begun to penetrate their mindset.

   To be honest, the explanations offered above are more detailed
and penetrating, more revealing of worldview, than what the traveler would normally pick up from engaging with the locals, no
matter how astute and culturally self-aware they might be. These
explanations are only intended to illustrate what we mean by worldview or mindset and thereby to suggest in a general way what awaits
the traveler who probes the psyche of the locals. If we consider that
this example only follows the trail of one encounter with difference back to its source, imagine what the traveler stands to learn by
repeating this process numerous times in the course of the voyage.

Engaging with the Locals

   The portion we see of human beings is very small:
   their forms and faces, voices and words, their ages

and race perhaps: beyond these, like an immense dark continent of which their obvious self is but a jutting headland, lies all that has made them.

Freya Stark
The Journey's Echo

But probing the psyche of the locals is much easier said than done, much more than a matter of going overseas and rubbing elbows with foreigners. In that respect, it differs from the other two processes described in these pages: learning through observing the foreign place (chapter 2) and learning through observing the natives in action (chapter 3). In both cases, that learning is more or less automatic and largely passive; it is built into the travel experience. But cracking the local worldview is not automatic; it requires deliberate and persistent effort. There are no guarantees, in other words, that mere proximity to the locals will result in penetrating their mindset. It all depends on what you do with that proximity. Another worldview *is* there for the taking when you go abroad, *but you have to take it.*

So just how is the traveler supposed to get inside the head of the locals? This gets us into a discussion about how to travel, which is the subject of our next chapter. Suffice it to say here that the traveler has to talk to the natives, engaging with them as often as possible, working out conscious, deliberate strategies to put himself in their path whenever circumstances permit. It means spending time in the places where they spend time and not in places where only foreigners and tourists go. It means riding the buses and trains the locals ride and going to the shops and services they go to. It means traveling slow and creating the conditions to meet people. In the end, it means doing whatever it takes to get into conversations with foreigners. "This is the only way," Lord Chesterfield declared, "of knowing the customs, the manners, and all the little characteristical peculiarities that distinguish one place from another; but then this familiarity is not to be brought about by cold formal visits of half an hour; no, you must show a willingness, a desire, an impatience, of forming connections" (Massingham and Massingham, 4).

A Worldview Sampler

And once connected, what should the traveler and the locals talk about? In the long run, it doesn't matter. Any exchange with the locals on virtually any subject is bound to reveal some of the values and beliefs that inform their worldview, if only indirectly. Even so, we can suggest a few themes the traveler could keep in mind, what we might call the building blocks of worldview—the fundamental dimensions or categories of the human experience concerning which different cultures have evolved very different perspectives, leading, ultimately, to very different notions about what is normal and what is not. Being aware of these will help the traveler know what to listen for in conversation with the locals, perhaps even what to ask about. Moreover, knowing about these concepts prepares the reader for our final subject in this chapter: the consequences of encountering a new worldview.

Building Blocks of Worldview

DIMENSION	ONE PERSPECTIVE	THE OPPOSITE PERSPECTIVE
Locus of Control	**Internalist:** • An activist mentality • What happens in life is up to you • You control your own destiny • There is nothing you must just accept and cannot change • The only limits to what you can achieve are internal (those you impose on yourself) • There is no such thing as luck; you make your own luck • Life is what you do	**Externalist:** • Stoicism, fatalism • Some things are not meant to be, cannot be changed, and must be accepted • Some things cannot be achieved no matter how hard you try • Some limits are real, external, and not self-imposed • Possibilities may be circumscribed • Luck or good fortune determine the outcome of some undertakings • Life is in part what happens to you
Concept of Identity	**Individualism:** • Emphasis on personal fulfillment and self-realization • Self-reliance and independence are highly valued • Important to be able to "stand on your own two feet" • Self-esteem is in part a function of what you have accomplished, what you have "done" with your life	**Collectivism:** • People rely on and cultivate the good wishes and sufferance of others • The success of the group guarantees the well-being of the individual • Personal fulfillment is often sacrificed for the greater good of group harmony and cohesion • People are relationship-oriented because good relations ensure superior results

DIMENSION	ONE PERSPECTIVE	THE OPPOSITE PERSPECTIVE
Concept of Identity (Cont.)	• Competition is more common than cooperation • People are more task-oriented • "Nice guys finish last"	• It's not where you "finish" that matters but how you get there
Concepts of Right & Fairness	**Universalist:** • People live in a black-and-white moral/ethical universe • What is right is always right, regardless of circumstances, and what is wrong is always wrong • To be fair is to treat everyone the same • How you are treated does not depend on who you are or who you know • No one is above the law • Everyone has the same opportunities—or at least they should • People do not expect and do not receive preferential treatment • People can be trusted until they prove otherwise • Life may not be inherently fair, but we can make it fair	**Particularist:** • People live in an ingroup/outgroup universe • How you treat others—what is right or wrong in any situation—depends on whether they belong to your ingroup (family, extended family, a small circle of friends), towards whom you have extensive and reciprocal obligations and responsibilities or whether they belong to the outgroup (everyone else) towards whom you have no obligations and who have none toward you • To be fair is to treat your ingroup very well and not worry about the outgroup • Laws and regulations are bent for the ingroup • The outgroup is automatically not trusted • Life is not fair

	Unlimited Opportunities:	Limited Opportunities:
Concept of Limits	• Resources, hence opportunities and possibilities, are unlimited • Everyone can have as much/be as successful as they want if they are willing to make the effort • The only real limits are internal, self-imposed • One person's success is not at the expense of someone else • Whatever you have or have achieved, you can always have/achieve more • "Failure" is for lack of trying (or drive) but not lack of opportunity • Everyone can be a winner • You always get another chance	• The "pie" is only so big, and its limits are fixed • There is a finite, limited amount of possibility, opportunity, limits to how much you can have or achieve • Not everyone can have as much/be as successful as everyone else • One person's success must come at someone else's expense • Not everyone can be a winner • Some people will lose no matter how hard they try • People cling tightly to whatever opportunity they get, however modest • You don't get a second chance
	High Tolerance:	**Low Tolerance:**
Attitude Toward Risk	• Risk is a fact of life, built into almost any situation • It's not possible to factor all risk out of most decisions/actions • You can't know anything for sure until you try • Nothing is ever perfect the first time (and we can always fix it later) • Making mistakes is how we learn; some mistakes can't be avoided	• Taking risks and failing have strong negative consequences • You should not have to take chances if you do your homework • Most risks (and their consequences) can be avoided if we do enough analysis and gather enough data • Risk-taking is for those who are impatient or just lazy

DIMENSION	ONE PERSPECTIVE	THE OPPOSITE PERSPECTIVE
Attitude Toward Risk (Cont.)	• There's always a better way of doing something • Tradition is not valued for its own sake • "The way we have always done things" can always be improved • What is new is not threatening • Failure and setbacks are only temporary	• Most mistakes can be avoided with careful planning • There is no need to "fix" something if we take the time to get it right in the first place • Tradition should not be lightly thrown aside • There are good reasons for "the way we have always done things" • What is new is unproven and should be approached with healthy skepticism • The consequences of failure and setbacks are not easily overcome
Concept of Time	**Limited:** • There is a fixed amount of time—and never enough • People are highly sensitive to time and use it as efficiently as possible • To be late is to waste people's time, so late is defined as just a few minutes • Deadlines and schedules (which impose control on time) are sacrosanct • Long-term means one or two years • Time has to be divided among all the people to whom one owes one's time (which is potentially everyone in a universalist culture, see above)	**Unlimited:** • Time is fixed and limited, but it never feels like that because these are particularist cultures (see above) where you only owe your time to a circumscribed universe of individuals: i.e., your ingroup • You always "have time" for these people, and you frequently do not have time for outgroup members (who likewise may not have time for you) • Everyone understands if you are "late" because it must mean you are spending time with other key ingroup members (being "late," in short, doesn't necessarily mean you will

Concept of Time (Cont.)		
	• On occasion people might not "have time" for their friends (and friends will understand) • People tend to be monochromic, believing it is more efficient to do one thing at a time/wait on one person at a time (hence, queues)/complete one task before starting another • The demands of time sometimes take precedence over the needs of people	• Deadlines can always be adjusted for "friends" • The long term is 20 years or more • People tend to be polychronic, effortlessly juggling several tasks/waiting on several people at once (hence no queues) • The needs of people (ingroup) always take precedence over the demands of time

View of Human Nature	Benign:	Skeptical:
	• People are inherently good, and they should be trusted until they prove otherwise • They can normally be counted on to be fair and play by the rules • On the whole people do not try to take advantage of each other • You can usually take people at their word • People should be given the benefit of the doubt • It is cynical to always look for the "trick" or to doubt anything that seems too good to be true	• People are not inherently good or bad, but you should never trust other people without good reason • People cannot always be counted on to be fair or play by the rules • People will take advantage of you if given a chance, so you have to protect yourself • Skepticism is advised • It's naïve to think you can take people at their word • Things that look too good to be true usually are

DIMENSION	ONE PERSPECTIVE	THE OPPOSITE PERSPECTIVE
Communication Style	**Direct:** • Plain-speaking and being more explicit—saying what you mean and meaning what you say—are valued • People tend to interpret messages literally and not read between the lines • The whole point of communication is to say what you're thinking • Telling the "truth" is more important than just saying what other people want to hear • Saving face is not valued above "being honest" • Words are the primary carrier of meaning • Nuance and understatement are deemphasized • What you say in public (e.g., at a meeting) should be very close to what you say in private, one-on-one • "Yes" means yes	**Indirect:** • Being implicit, suggesting, using nuance and understatement are all highly valued • People try to say what will allow them and others to save face and/or what they think the other person (especially someone older or senior) wants to hear • The message is often contained in what is not said (so you have to read between the lines) • The whole point of communication is to preserve and strengthen personal relations • If the "truth" would hurt, then something less unequivocal/more nuanced is appreciated and/or expected • People try to avoid public disagreements (e.g., in meetings) and may say one thing in front of others and something else one-on-one • "Yes" does not always mean "yes"

These, then, are some of the dimensions of worldview, the origins or starting points of behavior. Using the chart, we might consider two examples of how worldview influences behavior. If we look at the communication style dimension, we see that people in an indirect culture place a high value on saving face, and therefore when someone makes a mistake in that culture, it would be normal behavior to point this out somewhat tactfully, by saying something like "Is that really what you intended?" And even then such a correction would typically take place one-on-one and not in front of others, such as at a meeting, for example. But someone from a more direct culture that values plain-speaking and does not place any particular value on saving face would correct a mistake by saying something like "I don't think that's right" or even "That's wrong." And it would even be appropriate, in many cases, to offer this correction in front of others.

Or let's say people come from what is sometimes called a collectivist culture (the concept of identity dimension) where group harmony is more highly valued than individual fulfillment. In such a culture, parents would probably praise a small child who remains silent when her older brother steals her toys (although they would most likely discipline the boy later). In a more individualist culture, which values self-reliance, the parents would admonish the girl as follows: "Don't let your brother bully you like that. You've got to learn to stand up for yourself." The link between worldview and specific behaviors is not hard to see.

There are many other dimensions of worldview, of course, other categories of the human experience, and different commentators will often have different ways of describing the same dimension, but the two examples given above should suffice for our purpose here, which is to illustrate what awaits the traveler who follows the behavior of the locals back to its source. It should not be difficult for the traveler (or for the reader) to grasp that an internalist, individualist, universalist, time-deprived, plain-speaking risk-taker lives in a very different world from an externalist, collectivist, particularist, time-rich, understated risk-evader. Seeing inside that other world is the ultimate prize of serious travel.

The Holy Grail

> If you have been reared in the belief that your own country, or your own state, town, or hamlet, contains all that is good in the world, whether of moral excellence, mental development, or mechanical skill, you must prepare to eradicate that belief at an early date.... To an observant and thoughtful individual the invariable effect of travel is to teach respect for the opinions, the faith, or the ways of others, and to convince him that other civilizations than his own are worthy of consideration.
>
> Thomas W. Knox
> *How to Travel*

Thus far in this chapter we have described the fundamental link between behavior and worldview, given a detailed illustration of how the way people think affects what they say and do, and provided a brief sampler of worldviews. Our final task here is to describe the effects on the traveler of successfully penetrating an alien mindset, completing our answer to the question that inspired this project and informs these pages: How do individuals by travel enlarge their mind and add to their personality?

But first we need to recall where we last saw the traveler and what he was doing. He was moving about the new country, observing and being regularly jolted by the behavior of the locals, and he had come to the realization that they danced to a very different tune. Moreover, he accepted that these sounds are unquestionably music to local ears even if they are all dissonance to his. In short, faced with the reality of an entire population behaving the same odd way, our traveler has been forced to conclude that he has not in fact fetched up in a nation of crazies but that the seeming craziness all around him is the local version of normal. He had never known there were *versions* of normal, of course—heretofore, there had always been normal and not normal—and that discovery has begun to change his life.

One of the greatest changes resulting from penetrating a foreign mindset is the realization that most people behave logically most of the time. You may not approve of their logic or appreciate all the behaviors it leads to, but once you see the reasons behind the things people say and do—once you realize that there *are* reasons behind their behavior—you begin to accept that it makes sense. And you also realize something else, perhaps not right away and probably not consciously: sooner or later it occurs to you that if you can even *begin* to penetrate a foreign worldview, begin to see logic where there was only surprise and confusion, then that has to mean that it is actually possible to understand people entirely unlike yourself. To be sure there will always be people you *do* not understand—so long as there are cultures and worldviews you have yet to encounter—but you now know that there will never be people you *can*not understand.

And that realization makes the world a very different place. Why? Because it's human nature to mistrust and be afraid of what we do not understand, and especially of people we do not understand. Naturally, we don't all go around in a state of constant fear and agitation because there are so many foreigners out there. But is there any doubt that we are all most comfortable, most at ease, among people like ourselves, people we instinctively understand and who we know instinctively understand us? There may be no guarantees of absolute safety in the world, but surely the closest we can get is to be surrounded by people we understand.

When we travel and encounter people we do not understand, and then we engage with such people and begin to fathom their mindset, the experience of seeing the world from their point of view is immensely liberating. Knowing as you now do that it is possible to make sense of what is strange and incomprehensible— because you have just done it—means you need never again be afraid of what you do not understand. When you are no longer afraid of difference, you can always find a way to live at ease among people who are nothing like you.

But this does not mean, incidentally, that you have to approve of or start subscribing to all the odd worldviews out there. Where do I sign up? And it certainly doesn't mean that once you see where foreigners are coming from, then you have to accept all the behaviors that go along with their worldview. Understanding does not always lead to acceptance. That inveterate traveler Aldous Huxley, even as he champions the life-changing potential of travel, cautions us against an unthinking embrace of all that is foreign in a fit of reverse xenophobia.

"Convinced by practical experience of man's diversity," he observes,

> the traveler will not be tempted to cling to his own inher-
> ited national standard as though it were necessarily the

only true and unperverted one. He will compare standards; he will search for what is common to all; he will observe the ways in which each standard is perverted, he will try to create a standard of his own that shall be as free as possible from distortion…a standard of values that shall be as timeless, as uncontingent on circumstances, as nearly absolute as he can make them. Understanding diversity, he will tolerate it, *but not without limit.* He will distinguish between harmless perversions and those which tend to deny or stultify the fundamental values. Towards the first he will be tolerant. There can be no compromise with the second. (1985, 208; italics added)

To be sure, we must make every effort not to judge until we understand. But once we do understand, we must not shrink from judging, lest we deny our humanity. With regard to some aspects of "an alien culture," the novelist Hilary Mantel has observed, "you must not automatically respect it. You must sometimes pay it the compliment of hating it." To understand is not always to forgive.

Another effect of penetrating a foreign mindset is that it gives the traveler a new perspective, an additional vantage point from which to observe and try to make sense of the world and himself. An internalist (see earlier chart) understands the world one way, an externalist a different way; someone who has been exposed to both perspectives has two ways to make sense of his experiences, two frameworks for analyzing and understanding human behavior. In short, what cannot be understood from one perspective, from one set of life experiences, can sometimes be understood—or more fully understood—from another. "What matters," Dan Kieran has written, "is being aware that other ways of 'knowing' exist. Given the way the brain makes sense of the world, the different cultures and ways of knowing...are surely what we are all ultimately looking for when we travel" (186).

Moreover, having multiple perspectives on anything enables comparison, comparison enables evaluation, and evaluation enables choice. When the traveler understands several worldviews, several different ways of thinking and the behaviors they produce, he may discover that he admires or feels a natural affinity for certain aspects of a foreign worldview, that he feels more comfortable with certain values, behaviors, or attitudes he finds abroad than those he acquired in his own culture. And he may wish to integrate portions of these alternatives into his own personality and lifestyle going forward. Norman Douglas compared the phenomenon to "those paper flowers...we used to put in our finger-bowls at country dinner-tables. They look like shriveled specks of cardboard. But in the water they begin to grow larger and to unfold themselves into unexpected patterns of flowers of all colours. That is how I feel—expanding and taking on other tints.... [N]ew influences are at work upon me. It is as if I needed altogether fresh standards" (186).

Being exposed to a different mindset also brings the traveler in touch with his own mindset, his own way of thinking, continuing that inner journey we have referred to so often in these pages. As we try to work out how the locals think, our own ways of thinking come into sharper focus. It is one of the great ironies of travel: the more we are exposed to difference, and the greater and more numerous the differences we are exposed to, the more comparisons that are triggered with home; the more we compare abroad to home, the more clearly home stands out in contrast; and the more clearly we see the place we come from, the better we understand who we are. We go abroad to encounter the natives, and we end up meeting ourselves.

I often think back to my time in Morocco, where I was a Peace Corps volunteer teaching English in a secondary school. It is the custom there for all the students to stand when the teacher enters the classroom. Being a deeply egalitarian American, believing that everyone is equal and no one is better than anyone else, I found this display of deference quite uncomfortable, and I told my students not to stand when I came in. And of course I had serious discipline problems for many weeks. There was nothing I could do about this problem that first year, but at the start of my second year, with all new students, I let everyone stand.

The experience exposed something I had never realized, how instinctively Americans react to behaviors that draw attention to rank, how sensitive we are to even the subtlest indicators of inequality. These sentiments are natural enough in a country founded by people who suffered mightily from and were determined to escape a deeply unequal feudal system. But this is not something I had ever understood about myself until that first morning in Lycee Hassan II in Safi when all my students stood for me.

It made me think: Why did my students stand? Did they somehow believe I was better than they were? And if so, for it certainly seemed that way, was that really as abhorrent as I thought? Wasn't I better? If I wasn't better, better at understanding and teaching English anyway, then why was I standing at the front of the room? Weren't they just showing respect for my superior knowledge and my teacher training? Didn't this standing up really mean I had a deep obligation to be the best teacher I knew how to be? A responsibility to do everything I could to deserve this respect? I have never thought of egalitarianism the same way since.

Surely the possibility of meeting ourselves accounts in part for that most fervent wish of all the great travelers: to go to a place as different as possible from home. The more different the places we go to, the more we will add to our understanding of who we are. "Each time I go to a place I have not seen before," Paul Bowles has written, "I hope it will be as different as possible from the places I already know" (1984, vii).

In his book *Journey to Kars*, Philip Glazebrook notes that "visitors to Turkey at all times have been concerned to feel as strongly as possible the alienness of the place.... It is to feel the outlandishness of abroad that I leave home—to feel the full strength of its distinctive foreign character *and to come to terms with that*" (183; italics added).

Some readers may be wondering why the inner journey has received so much attention in these pages. Why has self-knowledge been held out as such a great boon? For some people, it probably isn't; when they see more clearly who they are, they may be quite content with the view, in which case increased self-knowledge has not brought them any particular advantage. But for many others, when they see more clearly who they are, they may wish to be someone else, someone better; they may not like everything they see—some of their attitudes, for example, their habitual behaviors, their biases and prejudices—and may wish to change some things about their self. And thanks to travel, which has shown such a bright light on the traveler and his culture, the individual now has that self-awareness that is the starting point of all personal growth.

Moritz Thomsen describes just this kind of self-exposure in his book *The Saddest Pleasure*, about his travels in Brazil. "But this trip, which has scarcely begun," he writes, "has already changed me; certain aspects of my character have become magnified to an alarming degree...I detect vast capacities for impatience, resentfulness, anger and cynicism" (46).

In his many travel books, Huxley returns repeatedly to the theme of encountering new worldviews and of the transformative effect they have on the traveler:

> So the journey is over and I am back again where I started, richer by much experience and poorer by many exploded convictions, many perished certainties. For convictions and certainties are too often the concomitants of ignorance. Those who like to feel they are always right and who attach a high importance to their own opinions should stay at home. When one is traveling, convictions are mislaid as easily as spectacles; but unlike spectacles, they are not easily replaced. (1985, 206)

Exploded convictions and perished certainties are the legacies of true travel. And what wonders they are, for in their wake, in the inevitable void they leave behind, travelers are extraordinarily susceptible to new influences and fresh perspectives, to adding to their personality. Albert Camus observes how in such moments we are "feverish but also porous, so that the slightest touch makes us quiver to the depths of our being" (32).

In *The Gobi Desert* Mildred Cable uses a different image, but she too is describing how it feels when a new experience suddenly upends a deeply held belief. Imagining how the villagers of an isolated, remote town in the Gobi would feel if they ever came face to face with a new phenomenon, she writes that the people

> of Chihkin were so convinced that their way was the only right one that their minds were barricaded as effectively by prejudice as their citadel was by stone walls. The opening of

a fissure through which a new thought might find entrance to the mind would be more terrifying than a sudden crack and collapse of the stone battlement which safe-guarded them from the enemy. (29, 30)

They may be terrifying and unsettling and even make us fever-ish, but shattered convictions and abandoned certainties are to be cherished, for they prove to us beyond any doubt that we can change. And if we can change, we can grow.

And people who can grow are humanity's best hope.

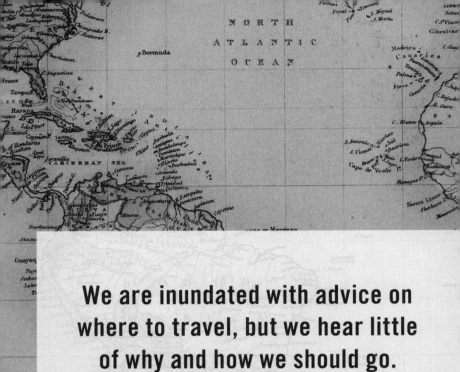

We are inundated with advice on where to travel, but we hear little of why and how we should go.

Alain de Botton
The Art of Travel

CHAPTER 5

How to Travel

We began this project with the somewhat bold declaration that "travel offers unparalleled opportunities for self-improvement and personal growth." Then we spent four chapters backing up this claim, hoping readers who liked what they heard about travel would be inspired and take to the road. If you are such a reader, then perhaps you will appreciate some advice on how to make the most of your journey.

The Life Lessons of Travel

But first let's pause here for a moment to collect in one place the various conclusions regarding travel strewn about the previous chapters. Our aim in these pages was to answer the question we posed in our introduction: How does travel change the traveler? And here is what we have learned.

1. You realize the impact of place, of physical surroundings, on how people think and act, and you begin to understand how your own place has molded you.
2. You accept that there are varieties of normal and that what is different need not be threatening.
3. You learn how easy it is to misunderstand others and the folly of judging—and especially of *acting*—before you understand.
4. You realize it is possible to understand what appears to be altogether foreign and that you need not fear what is merely different.
5. In learning about another culture and worldview, you see your own culture and yourself in new ways.
6. Your ethnocentrism comes under withering attack and begins to unravel; you acquire the capacity to grow.

An embarrassment of riches, to be sure, but the truth is that travel, if done right, can actually deliver on these extravagant promises. You must observe closely, of course, with all your senses alert. But even then these marvelous results will not all appear immediately. The seeds of these realizations are certainly planted during the journey, as part of the encounter with difference, but they will mature at various rates. You will have some of the insights listed above while still abroad, others only after returning home, and still others may require more travels (and other experiences) before coming fully into their own. Some seeds may never develop beyond vague intuitions, while others will grow into conscious realizations. And there are numerous other variables that will determine in which ways and how profoundly you will be changed by your journey. But one thing is certain: however important the soil and the water, without the seed there can be no plant.

"Travel is an evolving experience," Dan Kieran writes. "It's tucked up there in your memory and when you need a bit of it, or a new perspective on something hidden within it, it will emerge into your conscious mind" (165).

A Word about Language

> "It's a funny thing; the French call it a *couteau*, the Germans call it a *messer*, but we call it a knife, which is after all what it really is."
>
> Richard Jenkyns
> *The Victorians and Ancient Greece*

Before we get to our advice, we have one more modest digression. Some readers may be wondering if we are assuming they know the local language when they travel. Rest assured we are not. While many people around the world, both travelers and locals, speak English (or at least some English), we recognize that most travelers are not able to speak the primary language of the countries they go to, and most natives likewise do not speak the traveler's mother tongue. Readers who subscribe completely to the logic of this book—especially to the need to uncover the foreign worldview, and who are accordingly keen to follow the guidance served up here—such readers may be forgiven for wondering what's the use of all this advice if we can't communicate with the natives?

To begin with, you don't need to speak the local language to experience the place—all the sights, sounds, smells of a foreign country (chapter 2)—and you likewise don't need the language to observe the behavior of the people (chapter 3). The problem comes with chapter 4 where the idea is to engage the local people in conversation to discover their values and beliefs, how they think, and why they behave the way they do. This requires probing beneath the surface, well beyond what can merely be observed; it requires talking and listening, two activities that depend almost entirely on knowing the local language.

It's possible to have these kinds of exchanges without knowing the local language, but such conversations and the relationships they lead to will necessarily be restricted to locals who speak English, usually as a second language. In most countries, these English-speaking individuals will belong to one or more subsets of the general population, usually people who are better educated and those whose work involves considerable interaction with foreigners. While you may thus be somewhat limited as to the variety of locals you can talk to, there is no reason to assume that individuals from these two demographics cannot be insightful interlocutors. Indeed, well-educated informants are more likely to have traveled and may be especially astute observers of culture. "Abroad, the people you end up talking to are usually the people who speak English," Thomas Swick has written,

> an ability that in most countries sets them apart from the general population. This is not a negative; it's the citizens who stand outside the society—often creative, artistic types—who have the best perspective on it [and] who can teach you the most. (59)

If not knowing the local language limits the types of foreigners you can interact with, it need not in any way limit the quality of the exchanges.

How to Travel

The time has come to offer some advice on how to travel: a few suggestions on how to execute your voyage so as to maximize your chances for personal growth and self-improvement. The careful reader will have seen much of this advice coming, emerging out of the analyses of how travel works its changes on the individual. But while much of the advice offered here can perhaps be inferred from earlier discussions, the time has come to be explicit.

1. Travel alone.

> The greatest travellers travel alone. They may hire guides, porters, or camel-drivers; they may join caravans or other groups of local people, either for safety, or for greater economy or to keep them company along the way; but they bring no fellow-countryman with them, believing—rightly—that such a companion would come between themselves and the land through which they are passing, cushioning them from its impact and, as it were, desensitising their antennae.
>
> John Julius Norwich
> *A Taste for Travel*

Apart from the great travel-vs.-tourism debate, few topics in all the literature of travel have evoked as much discussion as the matter of traveling companions. And for good reason; it's one of the most important decisions the traveler will make. But while the topic may indeed provoke considerable discussion, it provokes almost no argument, since there is demonstrably only one camp: the camp that says travel alone. Francis Bacon knew this back in 1625: "Let him sequester himself from the company of his countrymen," he advised the traveler, "and diet in such places where there is good company of the nation where he travelleth" (Norwich, 11). And no trustworthy travel writer since has ever maintained otherwise.

Why this insistence on going solo? To begin with, a companion greatly limits your freedom. You have to be sensitive to the other person's needs, interests, her stamina, her enthusiasms, and her worries. It's her journey as much as it is yours, and you must negotiate everything you do together: where to stay, where to eat, what time to begin and end the day, where to go (in the morning, after lunch, in the evening), how long to stay in one place, how to get from one place to another—choices with profound consequences for any journey but especially for serious travel.

And even the easiest, most flexible companion is bound to be a distraction. Her observations interrupt your thoughts; her mood affects your mood; her reactions to the foreign place affect how you see it; her opinions of the people may influence yours; you have to pay to attention to her conversation even as you're trying mightily to take in the world around you. Traveling companions "can mislead you," Paul Theroux writes. "[T]hey crowd your meandering impressions with their own; if they are companionable they obstruct your view. And if they are boring they corrupt the silence with nonsequiturs, shattering your concentration with, 'Oh, look, it's raining' and 'You see a lot of trees here'" (2011, 5).

Alain de Botton describes how subtly inhibiting it can be to travel with a companion. "It seemed an advantage to be traveling alone," he writes:

> Our responses to the world are crucially moulded by whom we are with; we temper our curiosity to fit in with the expectations of others. They may have a particular vision of who we are and hence subtly prevent certain sides of us from emerging. Being closely observed by a companion can inhibit us from observing others, we become taken up with adjusting ourselves to the companion's questions and remarks, we have to make ourselves more normal than is good for our curiosity. (252)

And the dangers of distraction and self-suppression aren't even the most important reasons to travel alone. The principal problem with traveling companions is that they can so easily isolate the traveler, coming between the traveler and the local people and thereby robbing travelers of the essence of the experience. This happens in two ways: a companion can get in the way of the traveler who is trying to reach out to the locals, and a companion can serve as a barrier to locals who might otherwise be inclined to reach out to the traveler.

Companionship, by its very nature, mitigates any urge the lonely traveler might otherwise feel to reach out and connect with others; if you have a companion, you're already connected, albeit not to a local. "The vulnerability of the solitary traveler," Eric Leed writes, "and the resulting fear make the traveler porous, needy, and alert to the possibilities of association" (234).

And when you do feel the urge to reach out, to meet the locals and engage them in conversation, it will always be harder if you are with someone else. You will almost always have a breakfast, lunch, or dinner companion; always have someone sitting next to you on the bus, the train, the subway, at the concert, the play, or the football game. Always have a companion at the museum or in the bazaar. There will always be someone who must either support you in your efforts to reach out, getting out of the way or gladly welcoming a third party to the conversation, or someone you will need to break away from or somehow reach past in order to connect with the locals. Either way, it is awkward.

In his book *The Idle Traveller*, Dan Kieran tells the story of a trip he and some friends took to Warsaw to attend a wedding. Kieran doesn't like to fly, so he took the train from London by himself while his friends flew out to Poland as a group. When he met up with them later at the bar of their hotel in Warsaw, he observed how they seemed completely unchanged by their trip, talking "about the same things we talked about at home. Their lives had barely been interrupted."

After the wedding Kieran's friends dropped him off at the train station for his return journey, "baffled" by his choice of conveyance. One hour into his train ride, Kieran befriended the Russian soldier sharing his cabin, who turned out to be a deserter from the army. As he listened to the soldier's fascinating story, Kieran imagined his friends "35,000 feet up in the air watching reruns of American TV shows—and I knew I would never travel that way again" (34, 35).

Companions also discourage the locals from reaching out to the traveler. Anyone who might want to connect with you, to sit down at your table or sit next to you on the bus, either cannot (the seat is taken) or has to break into your conversation. Put yourself in the place of a local: At one table in the café, two foreigners sit sipping their drinks, engaged in a lively exchange; at another table, a lone foreigner sits with her coffee, looking around, and perhaps even making eye contact with you. Which table would *you* approach?

Traveling with a companion inevitably means bringing part of your own culture with you, which only makes it that much harder to experience the foreign place. "Above all, a piece of Europe inevitably accompanied us," Ella Maillart writes, referring to her companion,

> through the mere fact of our association. That isolated us. I was no longer thousands of miles from my own world. I was not submerged by or integrated into Asia. Travelling in company, one does not learn the language so quickly. The natives do not make their own of you. You penetrate less deeply into the life about you. (46)

None of the foregoing is meant to suggest that if you can't travel alone, then don't bother. If solo travel is ideal in many respects, it is not always possible or realistic. Couples will want to travel together, of course, as will families in many cases. While they will not have all the same experiences as solo travelers, they will have many of them, and they will also have experiences that solo travelers cannot have. And all travelers—solos, couples, and families—can apply the remaining ten pieces of advice in this chapter.

In some cases, moreover, the right kind of companion can actually enhance the experience, even for serious travelers. If you are a shy person, for example, and find it awkward to reach out to strangers, then a garrulous, outgoing companion would be a great asset. A companion who speaks the local language could transform the entire experience. An adventurous companion could be the key to experiences a more timid traveler would never have. A companion with specialized knowledge—of history, architecture, art, local flora and fauna—can add a whole new dimension to your journey.

Traveling with a companion poses certain risks and is bound to transform the experience, but it does not have to diminish it. At the very least, the serious traveler should carefully consider the pluses and minuses of having a companion and make an informed, conscious choice.

In her great science fiction novel *The Left Hand of Darkness*, one of Ursula Le Guin's characters, an inhabitant of an alien planet, asks an emissary from Earth: "Why did you come alone?" "I thought it was for your sake that I came alone," the emissary replies,

> so obviously alone, so vulnerable that I could in myself pose no threat, change no balance; not an invasion but a mere messenger boy. Alone, I cannot change your world. But I can be changed by it. Alone, I must listen, as well as speak. Alone, the relationship I finally make, if I make one, is not impersonal, not political: it is individual. Not We and They...but I and Thou. (259)

2. Stay out of touch; go off the grid.

> Connection with home makes travel reassuring *and less intense.*
>
> Thomas Swick
> *The Joys of Travel*

Twenty years ago no one needed to be told to go off the grid; apart from expensive long-distance phone calls, there *was* no grid to speak of. Now in the Internet age of email, texting, Snapchat, Facebook, Twitter, and Skype, it's a simple matter not only to stay in touch with people back home but to be in touch in real time, instantaneously, from almost anywhere in the world. You can be admiring the splendid Greek temple at Sounion and simultaneously texting on your iPhone with friends back in Sioux City, Iowa.

Actually, that's just the point: in fact you *cannot* be simultaneously admiring the ruins at Sounion and text chatting with friends. You cannot *have* an experience and share it at the same time; any attempts at the latter are bound to diminish the former. To the extent you stay in close contact with people back home, whether instantaneously or only at certain times during the day, the impact of the foreign place on your consciousness will be lessened. If you bring home with you into a new country—issues you left behind; ongoing concerns about relationships, money, your work, family matters—it is bound to color your experience, distracting you at the very least, affecting your mood, and coming between you and the life around you. Virtual companions pose almost as great a threat to serious travel as real ones.

"After nine months in Provence, I was a different person," Thomas Swick notes.

Had Facebook and Skype existed then, the change would have been a lot less dramatic...because I would have spent a fair amount of my time engaged in former practices, cliques, mindsets. (And parochial ones, at that, since none of my friends were doing what I was.) My new life would have been pockmarked by incursions from my old one. Technology's ability to keep us connected would have hampered my growth. (80)

When you go off the grid, do it formally. Announce your intention to friends and loved ones, explaining that from this date to this date you will neither be checking for messages nor sending any. Otherwise, they might be worried when their emails or texts go unanswered. Making it official also means you won't be so tempted to fall off the wagon and look longingly at your electronic devices. And worst case, if you feel too lonely and isolated, you can always announce that you're back on the grid for the next 24 hours. But whatever you do, don't make your reappearance open-ended.

Going off the grid doesn't mean you don't want to share your experiences with your friends and loved ones. It simply means that you control the extent to which home can intrude upon and influence your adventure. If home is on your mind—because it is on the screen in front of you—then the foreign locale never has your full attention. Once you've made the eminently wise decision to travel alone, why would you turn around and bring everyone with you? "A degree of loneliness sharpens the perceptions wonderfully whilst travelling," Philip Glazebrook has written. "Alone you note everything and note, too, the effect of everything upon you. You are free to look hard and reflect in peace" (30).

3. Linger.

> All travelling becomes dull in exact proportion to its rapidity.
>
> John Ruskin

The idea will appeal instinctively to the serious traveler: the slower you travel, the more you will see. Indeed, traveling slow could almost be shorthand for much of the other advice in this chapter. "I do think it is this impulse to slow down that all travelers share," Dan Kieran writes in *The Idle Traveller*. "The thrill of living in the moment, which is the real destination of all journeys, is what the greatest travel writers are revealing in their meticulous descriptions of the places they go and the people they meet" (53).

Places reveal themselves slowly. Almost any scene you could observe overseas will change over the course of a few hours, revealing new details about the place and about how people use it. Think about it. You're driving in your rental car south from Errachidia toward Ouarzazate, on the desert side of the Atlas Mountains in Morocco, famous as "the route of the kasbahs." You might drive by a few kasbahs and see nothing but the buildings. Or you might stop at a kebab place just opposite a kasbah for a quick lunch and notice people coming and going, realizing for the first time that kasbahs are not merely picturesque architecture but also people's homes.

Or you might linger at the kebab restaurant for an hour or two, ordering mint tea and a pastry, keeping your eye on the kasbah. At first you might see children on their way to school; then, later, you might see an older woman carrying water jugs or an adult male leading a donkey loaded with palm fronds; and after that, the egg seller comes by on his bicycle. There's no telling what you might see, but one thing is certain: if you don't linger, you won't see anything. You can sit in one place all day and learn more about a country and its people than if you went to a dozen different locations.

Not only do you see more if you linger, you also increase your chances of getting into conversation with the natives. As you relax at the kebab restaurant, ordering refills, the owner, with nothing else to do now that the lunch hour has passed and the place is empty, may wander over and ask you if it's your first time in Morocco. You could inhale a quick coffee at the bar of a Paris café, swallow a croissant, and then rush off to the Eiffel Tower. Or you could take a seat, sip slowly, read a newspaper, and stay for two hours. After the morning rush, the waiter sits down to catch his breath (and have a cigarette, if it's Paris), glances over, and asks you where you're from. Or some of the other, post-rush hour, mid-morning crowd, some of the regulars—retirees, students— might sit next to you and chat you up. You never do make it to the Eiffel Tower, but you might learn something about the French. "The American who visits Europe for the first time," Thomas Knox wrote (in 1881), "is apt to be in a hurry and to endeavor to see too much....Instances have occurred of tourists who could not tell whether St. Paul's Cathedral was in London or Rome. Moral: Don't be in a hurry" (Knox, 23).

In the end, travel is not about how many places you see but how much you see of the places you visit.

4. Walk.

> Walking is the age-old form of travel, the most fundamental, perhaps the most revealing.
>
> > Paul Theroux
> > *The Tao of Travel*

"All horsepower corrupts," Patrick Leigh Fermor famously observed, reminding us that the pace at which we travel is as important as the places we get to (Kieran, 48). If the goal is to see as much as possible of a place and of what is happening around you, then the means of locomotion must be carefully chosen. And nothing meets the test better than walking. "I came to realize," Gardner McKay writes, "that I traveled best when I could travel no faster than a dog could trot" (Theroux, 2011, 15).

For one thing, walking puts you in complete control of your circumstances. You can go where you please and not merely where the bus or train or subway goes, you can go any time you please, and you can stay as long as you please. A related virtue of walking is that you can stop whenever you feel like it. If something engages your attention, you can stop and observe it. As the great Baedeker himself noted in his *Travel Guide to Britain* (1901), "The pedestrian is unquestionably the most independent of travellers" (Kieran, 78).

Walking also puts you in front of more locals than any other means of moving; you are in constant contact with locals if you are moving among them. And the slower you are moving, the greater your chances of interacting with the natives.

Perhaps the greatest advantage of walking is the slow pace at which the foreign place unfolds, how unhurriedly the scene passes by, thereby enabling you to see more—and to see more clearly—whatever is in your immediate surroundings. When you walk, every element of the scene has its moment, standing out in sharp focus, with all its details exposed. If you are planning to learn from the place when you go abroad, then the more complete your observations the better. But if you are moving at a pace even slightly

faster than a walk, you have only a matter of seconds to observe
the scene before it is gone, and even then it is more of a blur than a
proper sighting.

In *The Idle Traveller*, Dan Kieran writes about a trip across England in a milk float, an electric milk cart that moved at 5 to 10 miles
an hour. He and his friends weren't walking, but they were having
nearly the equivalent experience as far as their speed of travel was
concerned, and they reaped equivalent rewards. "We were travelling more 'deeply' than we would have done in our normal lives,"
he writes. From this experience Kieran realized that if your journey is just a blur of fleeting images glimpsed from a speeding car
or train, "you are not part of the country at all." Traveling at the
speed of a milk cart, on the other hand, he and his friends were not
only keenly aware "of the country we were travelling through—we
became part of it" (143–144).

Taken together, the advantages of walking guarantee a traveler the most complete experience possible of the foreign locale. "I
felt in touch with the country," Thomas Swick writes of a walk he
took across Poland to the shrine of the Black Madonna, "following
its paths, crossing its fields, kicking up its dust. I came to understand . . . that walking through a place, like writing about a place, is
a way to possess it" (17; paraphrasing Geoff Nicholson).

But walking is obviously not practical for traveling between
locations, unless the distance is less than five miles (in which case
the traveler might seriously consider walking). For longer dis-
tances, the serious traveler has three choices, each with its own
advantages: a rental car or a car with a driver, a bus, or a train.
They all move at roughly the same speed, although some trains are
quite fast. The advantage of a car is control: once again the traveler
can, within certain limits, decide where to go and how long to stay.

Hiring a car with a driver adds the element of traveling with a local and the opportunity of engaging the driver in conversation over an extended period of time, perhaps even days.

The advantage of buses and trains is traveling the way the locals travel and having them as your traveling companions. While the foreign scene passes by rather quickly, you have ample opportunity to get to know some of your fellow travelers. In places where boat travel is an option, the same advantages apply.

Flying is clearly a nonstarter for serious travelers. While it does offer the possibility of getting to know the person sitting next to you, it removes the element of place almost completely from your journey. You will undoubtedly cover distance when you fly, but you won't travel.

5. Every sight is a site.

> A travel book has the capacity to express a country's heart—and perhaps the heart of a traveler too—but only as long as it stays away from vacations, holidays, sightseeing and the half-truths in official handouts.
>
> Paul Theroux
> *New York Times Book Review*

The guidebooks and the TV travel shows are all about the famous sites: churches and temples, forts and castles, museums, bazaars, dramatic landscapes. These are the places (landscapes excepted) where you will learn about the history and culture of a foreign country. And while there is no reason to avoid these places, the serious traveler is a collector of sights, not sites.

After all, the sites are either dead or devoid of any locals. No one lives in the castle or the fort; no one is worshipping or getting married when the tourists wander through the cathedral; the museum is full of fellow travelers. Only the bazaar is alive, although even the bazaar tends to be free of any locals (except for merchants) at those times—mid-morning, after lunch—when travelers typically visit.

For the serious traveler, every place is a site. A café, a barbershop, the post office—they are all sites in the sense of places where the traveler is likely to see what he has not seen before and learn something about the foreign country and about his own. Indeed, the more unexceptional and mundane the place—the more typical and representative it is of everyday life—the more the traveler stands to learn from it. To tourists, such places are unremarkable, but to the serious traveler every place has something worth remarking. "There are not many born travellers," Freya Stark writes, "though they all think they are— but they never like the dull patches" (1976, 123). Dull patches, daily life unfolding in all its normality, are a gold mine for the serious traveler.

"A good traveller does not much mind the uninteresting places," Stark writes in another passage.

> He is there to be inside them, as a thread is inside the necklace it strings. The world, with unknown and unexpected variety, is a part of his own leisure; and this living participation is, I think, what separates the traveller and the tourist, who remains separate, as if he were at a theatre, and not himself a part of whatever the show may be. (1990, 47)

By all means, visit the museum, plug into the audio tour, and study the paintings and sculptures. Then stop by the museum coffee shop and start a conversation with the waiters.

6. Secure an introduction.

> Let [the traveller moving] from one place to another
> procure recommendation to some person of quality
> residing in the place
>
> Francis Bacon

Chapter 4 explained that the only way to learn about a foreign worldview is to get into conversation with the locals. While you can observe the place and how the people behave, you can't observe a worldview; you have to be told about it. That means talking to the natives.

But first you have to meet them; you have to put yourself in the path of the locals and create the circumstances that lead naturally to conversation. Indeed, much of the advice in this chapter, especially the items that follow, are aimed in part at just that eventuality, at increasing your chances of establishing some kind of relationship with selected foreigners.

But in some cases you may be able to do an end run around all these strategies and meet a foreigner with very little effort. If you think about it, there may be someone in your or your family's circle of relatives, friends, work contacts who knows someone in the country or countries you are planning to visit, someone they could contact on your behalf and arrange an introduction. It might be a business associate, a friend from college, a family met through an exchange program, the parents of your child's French teacher at school, or maybe the family of your next-door neighbors who emigrated years ago from Pakistan. You could then email this individual or family before you set out, making an initial contact, and follow up with an in-person meeting once you arrive overseas.

With one stroke, you have met a local and begun a relationship—before you have even left home.

Or perhaps you know someone who has recently been to the country you're planning to visit and still has the business card of the rug merchant in the medina or still remembers the name of the friendly waiter in the café in Bogota or the hotel clerk in Singapore. In these instances, you should take with you a picture of your acquaintance back home (or even the rug seller's business card) to remind the in-country contact who your mutual friend is.

Such arrangements will not always be possible, of course, and your friend at home would have to know her in-country contact very well before imposing you on that hapless local. But if such an introduction can be arranged, it essentially guarantees that you will meet at least one local when you travel. With or without such an introduction, you will still want to meet other locals, still want to consider the rest of the advice in this chapter, but having a local contact means you will arrive with the wind at your back.

7. Frequent the places where you'll find the locals.

> Nor did anyone find it strange that in a place where there were Hindu bhajans, Malay weddings and Shadow plays, and Chinese operas, the Club members' idea of a night out was a long drive to Singapore to see a British Carry On movie which they would talk about for weeks afterwards.
>
> Paul Theroux
> *The Consul's File*

If you want to meet a local, chances are you won't find her at the Roman ruins, at the museum, or at the restaurant in your hotel. "If I am faced with the decision of choosing to visit a circus and a cathedral, a café and a public monument, or a fiesta and a museum," Paul Bowles writes, "I am afraid I shall normally take the circus, the cafe, and the fiesta" (Theroux 2011, 260). Think of the places where you spend most of your time back home; that's where you're likely to find the natives. Granted, most of us spend most of our time back home at our workplace or in our house, two places travelers have limited access to, but there are other places travelers do have access to and where locals can also reliably be found.

While travelers might not normally think to frequent some of these places, they would not be considered out of place in them. Examples include the cinema, the theatre, the concert hall, and sporting events; the grocery store and most shops (except souvenir shops and other haunts geared to tourists); local parks and recreation areas (the beach, walking trails, even some gyms); *neighborhood* pubs, bars, cafes, and restaurants but not eating places in the city center, inside your hotel, or inside or near the major tourist sites. Travelers would not even be out of place in a local barbershop or hairdresser or a local church or house of worship (although mosques are usually not open to non-Muslims, except for mosques located in some Western cities, such as Paris or Washington, DC). "If you want to meet people," Thomas Swick observes, "you have to cross over into their world.... Instead of buying stamps with your postcards in the souvenir shops, go to the post office where waiting in line you get a real taste... of the life of a local" (61, 62).

The point is to be wary of the places deliberately set up to be convenient for travelers—any shop, service, or eating place inside or adjacent to a hotel—and the sites that make a particular destination famous: historical monuments, grand works of architecture, art museums. There's nothing wrong with any of these places, but if your goal is to put yourself in the path of the locals, these are not places the natives frequent. The writer Moritz Thomsen had the following rules for travel: "Dollar meals if I can find them; five dollar hotels if they still exist. No guided tours, no visits to historical monuments or old churches. No taxis, no mixed drinks in fancy bars. No hanging around places where English might be spoken" (38).

Writing of a trip to Istanbul, Paul Bowles describes "the importance of wandering" and of how as a wanderer he always tried "to get off the main arteries...and stay in the alleyways which are too narrow for anything but foot traffic" (another plug for walking). "These lanes occasionally open up into little squares...where [a] few Turks will be sitting about drinking coffee. Invariably, if I stop and gaze a moment, someone asks me to have some coffee, eat a few green walnuts and share his pipe" (2010, 123).

And Aldous Huxley makes three. "Everyone in the ship menaces us with the prospect of a very good time in India," he says of his voyage to Asia in the 1920s.

> A good time means going to the races, playing bridge, drinking cocktails, dancing till four in the morning, and talking about nothing. And meanwhile the beautiful, the incredible world [we've come to see] awaits our explorations, and life is short....Heaven preserve me, in such a world, from having a Good Time! I shall see to it that my time in India is as bad as I can make it. (1985, 11)

And one more thing: If you're going to turn up in local haunts, be sure to go there at the times the locals do: before work, at lunchtime, after work, and on weekends. Most people are at their desks mid-morning and mid-afternoon, the very times many travelers are most active.

8. Be a regular.

> This is the real utility of travelling, when by contracting a familiarity at any place, you get into the inside of it and see it in its undress.
>
> Lord Chesterfield
> *Letters*

A related piece of advice is to regularly eat and have a coffee at the same places, to become "familiar," as Lord Chesterton might put it. If you are spending a week in Mexico City, consider having your meals at one or two of the same places each day. Before long the waiters and waitresses will know you and start calling you by name, the first step in establishing a relationship. They may ask you what you did that day or where you're planning to go this afternoon or tomorrow, and from there the conversation—and the relationship—can go anywhere. But if you eat at a different place every meal, you will be a stranger wherever you go, and people will grant you the distance that is expected between two parties who do not know each other well.

Returning to the same shop every day—to buy juice, the newspaper, a pastry—can have the same effect. If you buy a carpet from a merchant in the souk in Marrakech on your first day in town and go back again the next day, it's guaranteed he'll start calling you Mr. Bob, ask how you slept, and send out for mint tea. By the third day, you'll be an honorary member of the family.

9. Get inside someone's home.

> You will meet with an abundance of stately receptions and of generous hospitality too in the East, but rarely, very rarely in those regions (or even, so far as I know, in any part of southern Europe) does one gain an opportunity of seeing the familiar and indoor life of the people.
>
> A. W. Kinglake
> *Eothen*

No doubt about it: the ultimate prize for the serious traveler is to be invited into a local's home. No other travel experience can teach you as much about the culture and the people than observing the home life of the natives. You will see how their houses are laid out, how people use the various rooms, what objects they own, how the different generations interact, how family members behave towards each other in some of their most private moments, and how guests are treated in the local culture.

If people are comfortable enough with you to invite you to their home, that usually means any conversations you have are likely to be less formal and more relaxed; you can inquire about a wider range of topics and probe more deeply than you can in casual, superficial conversations at a café or on the bus. But even without any conversation, observing people at home offers a window into their culture and worldview that few other travel experiences can match. "When the visitor has seen the [public plazas] and beaches and palaces," Paul Bowles writes, "he still has not seen [Tangiers'] most important single phenomenon, the one which gives reality to and determines the ultimate meaning of all the others: I mean the spectacle of the average Moroccan's daily life. This necessitates going into the homes…" (2010, 234).

I know what Bowles means. When I was in Morocco I became friends with a family who lived in the *medina* (the old town) in Marrakech; their son was a student of mine. I still remember the first weekend I spent as a guest in their home. I was assigned to the formal living room, and I was never left alone the entire time I was in the house. From time to time my minder changed, from the oldest son (my student) to his five-year-old brother, and many people in between. I appreciated their attention but I imagined that now and then I might be left on my own to read or perhaps take a nap. But there was always someone there, and I of course thought I had to be polite and talk to that person, which taxed my Arabic skills mightily and eventually exhausted me. Much later I learned that there had been no need for me to pay any but the most fleeting, cursory attention to my minders; they were not there to entertain me or engage me in conversation or even to keep me company. They were there, rather, because it would be rude to leave the guest alone lest he should need something. This was a wonderful insight into how guests are perceived in the Arab world.

But getting inside someone's home is easier said than done. Even in the most hospitable, most accessible of foreign cultures, people aren't in the habit of inviting complete strangers over for a meal. The trick, of course, is to become something *other* than a complete stranger. Hence, much of the advice already offered above: go alone, linger, take local transport, go where the locals go, become a regular. None of these strategies will guarantee an invitation, but they may pave the way for one.

And there are other options. An obvious one is to stay in a bed and breakfast rather than in a hotel. This doesn't automatically make you less of a stranger or otherwise guarantee you will become fast friends with your hosts or see that much of their house or family life, but it does put you in their dining room every morning and facilitates conversation.

Nor do you always have to befriend a local to score an invitation to their home; it may be enough to be the friend of a friend (see item 5). You may not know anyone well enough in the country you're visiting to merit an invitation, but someone you know may know a local. Before your trip, ask friends, associates, and relatives if they know anyone in Budapest, and then see if they are willing to arrange an introduction. In many cases, especially in Europe, the initial meeting is more likely to be in a café or a restaurant, in a public place, than in someone's home, but it can be the first step toward a home visit.

In the last few years, yet another avenue has opened up for getting inside people's homes: online "hospitality services" (Airbnb, crashpadder, roomft, VRBO, and others) connect travelers searching for alternative (non-hotel) accommodations with locals looking to rent or exchange rooms (beds but not necessarily breakfast). One such site advertises how guests "can build real connections with their hosts, gain access to distinctive spaces, and immerse themselves in the culture of their destinations."

10. Read about the country.

> [Travellers] need to read about the places they will
> visit, before, during, and after the journey.
>
> Robin Hanbury-Tenison
> *The Oxford Book of Exploration*

In many ways the most important learning that takes place during one's travels—penetrating the foreign worldview—is also the most difficult to pull off. To begin with, you can't see a worldview. You can be in a foreign country, scrupulously observing and reflecting on everything that comes at you—all the elements of place and the behavior of the people—and still not figure out how the locals think. You can certainly get hints from your observations and may even be able to intuit some aspects of the local mindset, but intuitions and best guesses are no substitute for real understanding.

A second problem is that even after you accept that observations alone can only get you so far, the only guaranteed route to worldview—i.e., getting to know the locals—is not especially straightforward (nor, for that matter, is it even guaranteed). Without an introduction, the traveler will have to make the kind of conscious, sustained efforts described elsewhere in this chapter merely to create the *possibility* of befriending a local.

Then there's the inconvenient fact that even after you've made a friend among the natives, you still may not have befriended a cultural informant. Some locals will be astute and reflective, quite capable of articulating how they think and why they behave the way they do, but others may not be nearly so self-aware.

Finally, there's the well-known paradox that the people who are from a particular culture are at a distinct disadvantage when it comes to explaining themselves. They don't think about their culture; they simply embody it. If they ever knew why they behave the way they do, which is unlikely, they have long since internalized their worldview, and the vast majority of their most common behaviors are entirely instinctive and automatic. They might be able to reconstruct the logic behind their actions if prompted, but only after considerable reflection.

All this should not discourage the traveler from reaching out to foreigners. It merely means that the traveler may want to supplement whatever insights he learns by engaging with the locals with other techniques for penetrating the foreign mindset. One of the easiest and best is to read about the local culture, either in travel narratives of the type quoted from in these pages (see Appendix C for recommendations) or in studies of individual cultures. Some of the best guidebooks may also contain information about values and beliefs.

Books, of course, can never be a substitute for the physical, emotional, and psychological impact of direct, firsthand experience; observations, for all their limitations, trigger responses and stimulate reflection in ways that reading never could. But reading can add invaluable perspective and meaning to direct experience, can confirm what travelers may only have inferred, and can add to and expand upon explanations and insights gleaned from informants. As we noted in chapter 1, experience is the raw material and the *sine qua non* of all knowledge, but it is not the same thing as knowledge. For knowledge, we can either wait for our experience to mature or we can read the writings of those in whom it has already matured.

There is something to be said for reading before the journey or even during, but the real payoff comes after the journey. The traveler has had all manner of experiences, some of which she has understood, some of which have been partially understood, and many of which remain a mystery. The passage of time, which is to say the addition of new experience, will help explain some of the mysteries of abroad, but the insights of the best travel writers can add immeasurably to our understanding of different worldviews.

11. Enjoy yourself

> I suppose there is something absurd about the intense happiness I get out of the simplest travel abroad....I must say I simply enjoy being alive.
>
> Guy Chapman
> *A Kind of Survivor*

Readers who have made it this far in this chapter could certainly be forgiven for thinking that travel sounds like a lot of work. Evidently it requires hours of plotting and scheming to get oneself in front of the locals, followed by earnest, intense conversations about the meaning of life, and finished off with considerable required reading. Sign me up!

If we have perhaps taken travel a tad too seriously in these pages, that's only because the natural tendency in our era is not to take it seriously enough, to commit tourism, in a word, and thereby miss many of the wonders of true travel. Be that as it may, it's still a trip, not a homework assignment. So even if you have been genuinely inspired by the possibilities for personal growth outlined in these pages, that doesn't mean you shouldn't enjoy yourself. Indeed, if you're not enjoying yourself, then you won't feel like traveling for very long.

Travel should never be a burden. You should not feel pressure to carry around the eleven items in this chapter as a kind of checklist of serious travel, making sure you tick off all the boxes. There is no need to choose between being a serious traveler and having a good time. On some days and on parts of others, you may feel like traveling with a bit more care and purpose; on other days, you may want to go to a historic site, chat with fellow travelers, or even have a quiet meal in your hotel room. Even the shortest of journeys can easily accommodate both of these moods.

When you get up every morning, then, don't think first about connecting with a local; decide, rather, what you would most enjoy doing that day, and then do it. But from time to time as you are doing that thing, whatever it is, you may also feel like incorporating some of the advice offered here. "I must admit," Freya Stark wrote, "that for my own part I travelled single-mindedly for fun" (Theroux 2011, 52). If the sainted Ms. Stark could permit herself to have a good time, then certainly the rest of us can.

When the Journey Is Over

> You will find me a savage, for I have seen and heard strange things, and they colour the mind. You must try to civilise me a little, beloved Domnul. I know that you will bear with me, but whether I can bear with England.…I come back…with a mind permanently altered.
>
> Gertrude Bell
> *The Desert and the Sown*

We have noted several times that the various fruits of travel mature at different rates. Some of the impact of travel is felt almost immediately, as soon as the traveler arrives abroad; some occurs during the journey; and much of travel's impact is not fully felt until long after the voyage.

We also spoke in these pages of an outer journey and an inner journey. Clearly, the outer journey ends when the traveler arrives back at her doorstep, but in many ways the inner journey, the rediscovery of home and of self, only intensifies at this point. "I always turn [to] the last page or two of a book of travels," Philip Glazebrook writes,

> even if I've only read bits of the book itself. When the traveller we've followed through remote scenes takes his latchkey from his pocket and runs up his own front steps, I want to know what is his view of his native land, how do things at home look to him through those eyes which have seen such events and adventures as he has recounted? Does the dingy snugness of England irk or gladden him, when he lands at Dover after months in such un-snug lands? Having crouched with him in the caravanserais of the East, I would like to sit beside him poking a coal fire in the waiting-room at Dover station, till a train takes us away up to London through the landscape of fields crowded in upon by fat trees, and watched over by thick-towered churches, so that I can hear his comments upon these homely scenes (241).

The traveler has been seeing home in her mind's eye, of course, almost from the first moments abroad, observing the foreign place from the perspective of home and vice versa. But now for the first time the traveler brings to bear directly on her homeland the enormous reservoir of new sensory memory accumulated on the overseas voyage. Everything the traveler sees back home is now seen anew, from an added perspective, and therefore seen more fully and more completely, with new dimensions and character-istics brought into sharper focus. The traveler sees home in ways she has never seen it before, in ways home *cannot* be seen from within, and with these new views come new comprehension and understanding.

As the traveler's perceptions of her physical surroundings flower and expand upon her return, her understanding of self expands simultaneously. The great lesson of the inner journey, after all, is how people are shaped by their place; the more one sees of one's place, therefore, the better one understands one's self. Even a single foreign voyage, if the voyager knows how to travel, can yield a lifetime of insight. Our friend Freya Stark surely had this notion in mind when she wrote: "There is this about love; that its memory is not enough, for the soul retracts if it does not go on lov-ing. Whereas to have travelled once, however long ago—provided it was real and not bogus travel—is enough" (2013, 77).

Homesickness is a feeling that many know and suffer from; I on the other hand feel a pain far less known, and its name is 'Out-sickness.' When the snow melts, the stork arrives, and the first steamships race off, then I feel this painful travel unrest.

Hans Christian Andersen

Our Insane Restlessness

Readers who have come this far might be wondering about the elephant in the room: we've managed to spend an entire book discussing the rewards of travel, but we have never once addressed the question of why people travel in the first place. This might be a good time.

As we have noted in several places, the essence of travel is encountering difference. So perhaps we can start there, with the assumption that although people travel for different reasons—for a change of pace, to get away, to relax, to forget, to see famous sites, to escape responsibilities and obligations—almost all travelers share a basic attraction to what is unfamiliar. As John Julius Norwich has observed, "For the true traveller the object of a journey is not pleasure, or comfort, or warmth, or sunshine. He is really travelling—even if he might not quite put it that way himself—in search of excitement, and challenge, and *the endless fascination of the unknown*" (10; italics added).

But why? Why do the exotic and the unknown excite us in ways the commonplace and the familiar never could? Why are we so drawn to what is different and unusual? Why does the mysterious exert such a strong pull?

A partial answer, surely, is that humans are naturally curious. But this does not completely satisfy and cannot be the last word. Why are we curious? What impulse are we responding to, what urge is it that overcomes us whenever we begin to feel the great unrest? Surely it's because we want to know more, to understand whatever can be understood. Which brings us, finally, to the core question: Why do we seek understanding?

Now we are in the realm of philosophy, somewhat beyond our brief in these pages, but we can hazard a few guesses. At some deep level in the human psyche, we are unnerved by what we do not understand, we feel vaguely threatened, unsettled. So whenever we read or hear about people behaving in ways that make no sense, that are contrary to everything we think of as rational and normal, we become ill at ease. These people can be on the other side of the world from us (they usually are) and in countries we will never visit, people who will never touch our lives in any way, but the very existence of members of our own species whose behavior defies all logic, whose actions, therefore, are impossible to predict, is profoundly troubling. It means we live in a world that is not altogether safe.

Perhaps we travel, then, for peace of mind. If we can find an explanation for those phenomena that appear to be inexplicable, a rationale for that which defies reason—not in every instance, in every place, but enough for us to see a pattern, enough to suggest that even the deepest mysteries can with time and effort be unraveled—then the world will hold fewer terrors for us.

Charles Darwin can perhaps help us here, too. He teaches that evolution selects for survival, for passing on those characteristics that ensure our overall safety and well-being. Any instinctive drive that reduces anxiety and leads to peace of mind, therefore, would be a most welcome addition to our DNA. In his modern travel classic *In Patagonia*, Bruce Chatwin describes a conversation he had in Chile "at the Estacion de Biologia Marina with a party of scientists.... The resident ornithologist was studying the migration of the Jackass Penguin. We talked late into the night, arguing whether or not we, too, have journeys mapped out in our central nervous systems; it seemed the only way to account for our insane restlessness" (83).

It's the final gift of travel: the reassurance that our fellow travelers on the planet, different as they are from us, different in some cases as it is possible to be from us, are variations on the human theme, but they are not an altogether different theme. How ironic that the urge to seek out the foreign and the unfamiliar originates, ultimately, in a deep desire to confirm that beneath the myriad differences between peoples lies a profound core of sameness. "The art of learning fundamental common values," Freya Stark writes, "is perhaps the greatest gain of travel to those who wish to live at ease among their fellows" (1988, 220).

Arthur Grimble, on the other side of the world from Ms. Stark, in the Pacific islands now known as Kiribati and Tuvalu, felt the same. "It began to dawn on me," he writes in his memoir *A Pattern of Islands*,

> that beyond the teeming romance that lies in the differences between men—the diversity of their homes, the multitude of their ways of life, the dividing strangeness of their faces and tongues, the thousand-fold mysteries of their origins—there lies the still profounder romance of their kinship with each other, a kinship that springs from the immutable constancy of man's need to share laughter and friendship, poetry and love in common. (2010, 20)

Perhaps our restlessness is not insane after all.

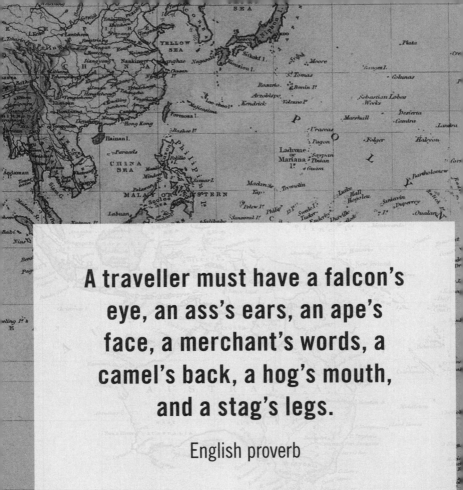

A traveller must have a falcon's eye, an ass's ears, an ape's face, a merchant's words, a camel's back, a hog's mouth, and a stag's legs.

English proverb

Rules for Travel

In chapter 5 we offered our rules for travel, but other and wiser souls have trod this path before us, in ages past and in the present (a number of whom we have quoted in other contexts in these pages). Here (in chronological order) we present a brief selection of these voices offering their considered advice on how to travel.

From Francis Bacon, *Of Travel*

1. He must have some entrance into the language before he goeth.
2. He must have such a servant or tutor as knoweth the country.
3. Let him carry with him also some card or book describing the country where he travelleth.

4. Let him sequester himself from the company of his countrymen and diet in such places where there is good company of the nation where he travelleth.

5. When a traveller returneth home, let him not leave the countries where he has travelled altogether behind him.

6. In his discourse let him be rather advised in his answers than forward to tell stories.

7. Let it appear that he doth not change his country manners for those of foreign parts but only prick in some flowers of that he hath learned abroad into the customs of his own country.

From Fynes Moryson (1617)

1. Do not trust chance companions on the road who, when they question you, should be told that you are going only as far as the next city.

2. Keep your temper if men try to quarrel with you.

3. Tell no one that you can swim for, in case of shipwreck, others trusting therein take hold of you and make you perish with them.

4. Always keep your sword at your side and your purse under your pillow.

5. If you also keep a book [under your pillow], make sure it is never one that might reveal your Protestant faith.

From Samuel Johnson, *A Journey to the Western Islands of Scotland*

I am much pleased that you are going on a very long journey, which may by proper conduct restore your health and prolong your life. Observe these rules:

1. Turn all your care out of your head as soon as you mount the chaise.
2. Do not think about frugality: your health is worth more than it can cost.
3. Do not continue any day's journey to fatigue.
4. Take now and then a day's rest.
5. Get a smart seasickness if you can.
6. Cast away all anxiety, and keep your mind easy.

This last direction is the principal; with an unquiet mind neither exercise, nor diet, nor physic can be of much use.

From Napoleon Bonaparte, *Napoleon's Letters* (addressed to his younger sister)

Make yourself remarked for your gentleness, your politeness to everyone, and an extreme regard for the ladies who are friends or relations on your mother's side of the family.

Above all, conform to the customs of the country. Never run down anything, find everything splendid; and don't say "We do this better in Paris."

Show great attachment and respect for the Holy Father, of whom I am very fond, and whose simple manners make him worthy of the post he holds.

The only foreigners you must never receive at your house, as long as we are at war with them, are the English—indeed you must never allow them to be in your company.

Love your husband, make your household happy, and above all don't be frivolous or capricious.

From Prince Hermann Puckler-Muscau, *Regency Visitor*

Had I to give a few universal rules to a young traveller, I should seriously counsel him thus: In Naples, treat the people brutally; in Rome, be natural; in Austria, don't talk politics; in France, give yourself no airs; in Germany, a great many; and in England, don't spit.

From Thomas W. Knox, *How to Travel: Hints, Advice, and Suggestions to Travelers by Land and Sea, All Over the Globe (1881)*

1. Close all your business and have everything ready the day before your departure.
2. Do not disturb yourself with unpleasant thoughts of what may happen [to transatlantic ships] in the fog.

3. When the ship is pitching violently in a head sea, avoid going forward on deck, as you may get a drenching unexpectedly and possibly may be washed overboard.

4. The moist climate of the British islands is apt to leave a disagreeable dampness on bed-linen and makes it very detrimental to the general health.

5. The American who visits Europe for the first time is apt to be in a hurry and to endeavor to see too much.... Instances have occurred of tourists who could not tell whether St. Paul's Cathedral was in London or Rome. Moral: Don't be in a hurry.

From Freya Stark, *A Winter in Arabia*

If I had to write a decalogue for journeys, eight out of ten virtues should be moral, and I should put first of all a temper as serene at the end as at the beginning of the day. Then would come the capacity to accept values and to judge by standards other than our own. The rapid judgement of character; and a love of nature which must include human nature also. The power to dissociate oneself from one's own bodily sensations. A knowledge of the local history and language. A leisurely and uncensorious mind. A tolerable constitution and the capacity to eat and sleep at any moment. And lastly, and especially here, a ready quickness in repartee.

From Dervla Murphy, *Full Tilt*

1. Choose your country. Choose guidebooks to identify the areas most frequented by foreigners—and then go in the opposite direction.
2. Mug up on history.
3. Travel alone or with just one prepubescent child.
4. Don't overplan.
5. Be self-propelled or buy a pack animal.
6. If assisted by a pack animal, get detailed local advice about the terrain ahead.
7. Cyberspace intercourse vitiates genuine escapism.
8. Don't be inhibited by the language barrier.
9. Be cautious but not timid.
10. Invest in the best available maps.

From Simon Raven, *Travel: A Moral Primer*

1. On arrival you are now your own master for up to three months. Do not abuse the privilege. Behave with modesty (especially if you are very young), lest you arouse curiosity.
2. Send frequent friendly postcards to your parents to forestall anxiety, but do not give too definite an impression of enjoying yourself, as this causes more irritation than anything else in the world.
3. Remember at all times that you are British. This is nothing to be ashamed of, nor... to be very proud of. But you

are what you are, and if you start pretending to be something else, you will become nobody at all.

4. When you go among foreign people, relish what is excellent and also take note of what is not.

5. [As] for their moral customs: accept them while there, understand them, imitate them if you wish. But be sure that you [do] not bring alien customs back to England.

From Pico Iyer (introduction to *The Skeptical Romancer*)

What makes a great traveler? The ideal [traveler] should be open to every person or encounter that comes his way, perhaps—but not too ready to be taken in by them. She should be worldly, shrewd, her feet firmly on the ground; and yet she should be ready to surrender, if only for a moment, to the magic and excitement of what she could never see or do at home. He should be curious, observant, funny, wry and kind.... [Great travelers are] rooted enough to be up for any possibility. They shouldn't have an agenda or overwhelming prejudices, and they should be able to see to the heart of the natives of any country as to their fellow travelers.

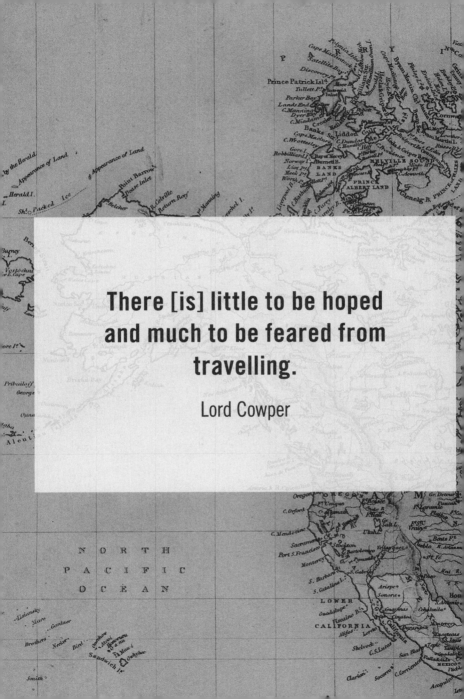

There [is] little to be hoped
and much to be feared from
travelling.

Lord Cowper

APPENDIX B

Not So Fast:
The Travel Cranks

Suffer not thy sons to pass the Alps.

Lord Burghley

Most of the evidence, literary and otherwise, supports the central theme of this book: that travel is uplifting and life-changing. Most, but not all. There are those travelers who did not feel especially lifted up by their experience and who would rather not have had their life changed, thanks anyway. In a nod to balance and fairness, we hereby present the views of the travel curmudgeons. Be prepared, incidentally, to find a few stalwarts here, travelers we have met elsewhere in these pages when, presumably, they were having a better day.

It's not altogether fair, meanwhile, to label these folks cranks and curmudgeons, as if to suggest they take their positions on travel just to be contrary rather than out of genuine feeling. We do apologize.

Is your journey really necessary?

Wartime British railway poster

What people travel for is a mystery. I have never during the last 48 hours had any wish so strong as to be home again.

Lord Macaulay
Letters

[We lament] the egress of our fools [to France] to glean up their vices, fashions, and frippery manufactures to the discouragement of our own arts at home and the disgracing of them in the eyes of all Europe.

London newspaper c. 1760

The great and recurrent question about Abroad is, is it worth the trouble of getting there?

Rose Macaulay
The Towers of Trebizond

Tourists are, in the main, a very gloomy looking tribe. I have seen much brighter faces at a funeral than in the Piazza of St Marks. One wonders why they come abroad. The fact is that very few travelers really like travelling.

Aldous Huxley
Along the Road

As you go along, you literally collect places. I'm fed up with going to places, I shan't go to anymore.

Bruce Chatwin
New York Times, 19 January 1989

But though every one travels in these days, just as every one reads, there are as few good travellers as there are good readers. The people who ask at lending libraries for the very newest book only to have to say 'they saw it, and liked it,' are precisely those who rush to and fro all over the earth, and return as empty as they set out. Travelling is either useful or not according to the motive with which it is undertaken. Some there are whose sole object is to get over a number of countries just to have to say they were in them. Such globe trotters neither improve themselves nor increase their happiness.

Rev. E. J. Hardy
Manners Makyth Man

When George V spoke of "bloody abroad," he was not entirely wrong; quite a lot of abroad is bloody in one way or another.

John Julius Norwich
A Taste for Travel

Many thanks for your letter, which a comfortable letter it was, but creates violent wishes to get back to England. For of *all the beasts* of countries I ever see, I reckon this about caps them.... How any professing Christian as has been in France and England can look at it passes me. A calcined, scalped, rasped, scraped, flayed, broiled, powdered, leprous, blotched, mangy, grimy, parboiled country *without* trees, water, grass, fields—*with* blank, beastly, senseless olives and orange-trees like a mad cabbage gone indigestible; it is infinitely liker hell than earth, and one looks for tails among the people.

Algernon Swinburne
Letters

This morning I feel a tremendous resentment against this country, and I withdraw from it desperately.

Andre Gide
Amyntas

I wouldn't mind seeing China if I could come back in the same day.

Philip Larkin

I shall stop as long as I can, and see all that can be grasped in the time, for I sincerely hope never to go abroad again. I never loved home so well as now I am away from it—and the exquisite sights which foreign countries supply both the imagination and the morsel taste are most pleasurable in *memory*, but scarcely satisfactory as present enjoyment. There is far too much of tumult in seeing the places one has read so much about all one's life to make it desirable for it to continue.

John Henry Newman
Letters

I loathe abroad, nothing could induce me to live there.... [As] for foreigners, they are all the same, and they make me sick.

Lord Redesdale
quoted in *Abroad*, by Paul Fussell

The truth is that I do not really like being abroad much. I want to see as much as I can this holiday and shut myself up for the rest of my life in the British Isles.

Evelyn Waugh
The Diaries of Evelyn Waugh

Since the days of Alexander the Great there has been a fashionable belief that travel is agreeable and highly educative. Actually, it is one of the most arduous yet boring of all pastimes and, except in the case of a few experts who go globe-trotting for special purposes, it merely provides the victim with more topics about which to show ignorance.

Sinclair Lewis
Dodsworth

Oriental scenes look best in steel engravings.

Mark Twain

We were buttonholed...by an animated professor, who was anxious to inform us that he had been given a year's holiday, with traveling expenses paid, to go wherever he liked, and that though only four months of it were over, he wished he was nowhere so much as back in Chicago, setting down to a good meal of buckwheat fritters and clams.

Robert Byron
in *Abroad: British Literary
Traveling between the Wars*

Farewell Madrid! I shall say of thee with the Portuguese poet:

He who likes thee does not know thee;
He who knows thee does not like thee.

Robert Southey
Letters

I told her that we had met with many things which we were anxious to see. 'I think this is just the notion, begging your pardon, that prevents people from ever taking a really long journey in proportion to the time they are about it. I, and my nephew, make a point of never stopping to look at things.'

Frances Trollope

What is the good of sending people around the world? I have done it: it doesn't help. It only kills time. You return just as unsatisfied as you left.

Ella Maillart
The Cruel Way

There comes a moment in the life of most travellers, I imagine, when they ask themselves, "What on earth am I doing here?"

Auberon Waugh

It is much better to read books of travel than to travel oneself; he really enjoys foreign lands who never goes abroad.

W. Somerset Maugham
The Land of the Blessed Virgin

When travellers take a delight in climbing mountains, I regard the mania as profane and barbaric.... These zig-zags and irritating silhouettes and shapeless piles of granite, making the fairest portion of the earth a polar region, cannot be liked by any kindly man.

Goethe (not enjoying the Alps)
Italian Journey

The very act of moving from A to an unknown B seems to bring out the best in authors. Some travel in order to write, some write because they have travelled, while others have such eye-opening experiences that it doesn't matter if they can write well or not. Even in the dullest, most dutiful Victorian tome you can usually detect some stirring of the soul.

Fergus Fleming
The Traveller's Daybook

APPENDIX C

Recommended Reading

Some readers and aspiring travelers may appreciate guidance on what travel writers and travel books they ought to read, either to prepare themselves for travel or to put past travel into perspective. All connoisseurs of the travel narrative have their favorite writers, but to make *this* list candidates have to meet two criteria: they have to write well, and their books have to be as much about the experience of travel as about the places visited. Their books have to contain reflection, in other words, and not merely description.

"The reader of a good travel book," Norman Douglas has observed,

> is entitled not only to an exterior voyage, to descriptions of scenery and so forth, but to an interior, a sentimental or temperamental voyage, which takes place side by side with that outer one. [T]he ideal book of this kind offers us, indeed, a triple opportunity of exploration—abroad, into the author's brain, and into our own. (25)

PAUL BOWLES was a famous American expatriate in Morocco, and from his perch there he observed and dissected the emotional and psychological impact of the foreign, publishing his conclusions in numerous short stories, several dark novels (*The Sheltering Sky, Spider's House),* and in numerous travel writings. Many of the latter are anthologized in *Travels: Collected Writings 1950–1993,* and then there is his masterpiece: *Their Heads Are Green and Their Hands Are Blue: Scenes from the Non-Christian World.*

ROBERT BYRON'S acknowledged masterpiece is *The Road to Oxiana,* but two other works—*First Russia, Then Tibet* and *The Station: Travels to the Holy Mountain of Greece*—are in the same exclusive league.

ANTOINE DE SAINT-EXUPERY wrote one classic: *Wind, Sand, and Stars.* Two other works—*Night Flight* and *Flight to Arras*—would be classics if they had been written by anyone else and did not have to be compared to *Wind, Sand, and Stars.* All three are collected in *Airman's Odyssey.* (He also wrote and is best known for *The Little Prince,* but it is not a travel book.)

NORMAN DOUGLAS wrote the best novel that has ever been confused for a travel book: *South Wind.* While it disappoints fans of fiction, it thrills fans of the travel narrative. Three other equally satisfying titles are *Old Calabria, Fountains in the Sand: Rambles Among the Oases of Tunisia,* and *A Dragon Apparent: Travels in Indo-China.*

PATRICK LEIGH FERMOR makes everyone's list, largely on the strength of his unfinished trilogy, beginning with *A Time of Gifts: On Foot to Constantinople* and followed up by *Between the Woods* *and the Water: From The Middle Danube to the Iron Gates.* He is a beautiful stylist and a sensitive observer.

PAUL FUSSELL was not a travel writer, but his book *Abroad: British Literary Travelling Between the Wars* is a brilliant analysis of the travel narrative and a short history of travel. It will also introduce you to some of the great British travel writers, including Robert Byron, Norman Douglas, Lawrence Durrell, Graham Greene, D. H. Lawrence, and Evelyn Waugh.

ALDOUS HUXLEY is most famous for his novel *Brave New World*, but he was a beautiful essayist and an inveterate traveler. If you read only one of his travel narratives, make it *Jesting Pilate*. If that pleases you, then move on to *Along the Road* and *Beyond the Mexique Bay*.

A. W. KINGLAKE'S *Eothen*, about a visit to the Holy Land in the 1840s, is a classic, but it's definitely not everyone's cup of tea. Many readers find it bold and amusing, and many others think it's smug and offensive. In the latter camp is none other than Edward Said who, in his landmark *Orientalism*, calls it "a pathetic catalogue of pompous ethnocentrisms" (193). Don't say you haven't been warned.

The name of **URSULA LE GUIN,** a master of science fiction, has only appeared once in these pages. But it might well have appeared more often, for what are the best works of science fiction if not novelized travel narratives, albeit with rather remote destinations? Le Guin is probably most famous for her *Earthsea* trilogy, but the two books the serious traveler should read are *The Left Hand of Darkness* and *The Dispossessed*. They are unparalleled evocations of what it feels like to be an alien in an alien culture.

FREYA STARK has been with us throughout these pages. She was prolific, with more than 20 titles to her name; the best known are probably *The Valley of the Assassins* and *The Southern Gates of Arabia,* but all of her books have the same qualities, making it difficult to recommend one over the other. Readers might start with an anthology of her work, *The Journey's Echo*, which includes excerpts from 15 different titles.

PAUL THEROUX has written 14 travel books (not including *The Tao of Travel*, see below) and more than 25 novels. He is a master of the "incident," encounters with the locals and colorful fellow travelers, and a keen and reflective observer. *The Great Railway Bazaar* launched his career; *Fresh Air Fiend* collects numerous other travel pieces.

Anthologies

Another way to decide who to read would be to dip into any of several excellent anthologies of travel writing. If you read an excerpt you like, you can always track down the source.

> *A Book of Traveller's Tales*, Eric Newby
> *A Taste for Travel*, John Julius Norwich
> *The Englishman Abroad*, Hugh and Pauline Massingham
> *The Norton Book of Travel*, Paul Fussell
> *The Oxford Book of Travel Verse*, Kevin Crossley-Holland
> *The Tao of Travel: Enlightenments from Lives on the Road*,
>   Paul Theroux
> *The Traveler's Daybook: A Tour of the World in 366*
>   *Quotations*, Fergus Fleming

Bibliography

Bishop, Morris. 1968. *The Middle Ages*. Boston: Houghton Mifflin.

Black, Jeremy. 2009. *The British Abroad: The Grand Tour in the Eighteenth Century*. Gloucestershire, UK: The History Press.

Bowles, Paul. 1984. *Their Heads Are Green and Their Hands Are Blue*. New York: Ecco Press.

Bowles, Paul. 2002. *Collected Stories and Later Writings*. New York: Library of America.

Bowles, Paul. 2010. *Travels: Collected Writings 1950–1993*. New York: Ecco Press.

Cable, Mildred. 1984. *The Gobi Desert*. London: Virago.

Camus, Albert. 2010. *Notebooks 1935–1942*. Lanham, MD: Ivan R. Dee.

Cantor, Norman. 1994. *The Civilization of the Middle Ages*. New York: Harper Perennial.

Carroll, Raymonde. 1988. *Cultural Misunderstandings: The French-American Experience*. Chicago: University of Chicago Press.

Chatwin, Bruce. 1977. *In Patagonia*. London: Jonathan Cape.

Condon, John C. and Fathi Yousef. 1985. *An Introduction to Intercultural Communication*. New York: MacMillan.

Davis, Norman. 1996. *Europe: A History*. New York: HarperCollins.

de Botton, Alain. 2002. *The Art of Travel*. Victoria: Penguin.

de Saint-Exupery, Antoine. 1967. *Wind, Sand, and Stars*. New York: Harcourt Brace.

Deutscher, Guy. 2005. *The Unfolding of Language*. New York: Henry Holt.

Douglas, Norman. 1987. *South Wind*. London: Penguin.

Durrell, Lawrence. 1957. *Bitter Lemons*. New York: E. P. Dutton.

Eisner, Robert. 1993. *Travelers to an Antique Land: The History and Literature of Travel to Greece*. Ann Arbor: The University of Michigan Press.

Espey, David. 2005. *Writing the Journey: Essays, Stories, and Poems on Travel*. New York: Pearson Longman.

Fagan, Brian. 2004. *The Long Summer: How Climate Changed Civilization*. New York: Basic Books.

Farrell, J. G. 1993. *The Hill Station*. London: Phoenix.

Fleming, Fergus. 2011. *The Traveller's Daybook: A Tour of the World in 366 Quotations*. London: Atlantic Books.

Freeman, Charles. 2002. *The Closing of the Western Mind*. New York: Vintage Books.

Fussell, Paul. 1980. *Abroad: British Literary Traveling Between the Wars*. New York: Oxford University Press.

Fussell, Paul, ed. 1987. *The Norton Book of Travel*. New York: W. W. Norton.

Gibb, Barry. 2007. *Rough Guide to the Brain*. New York: Rough Guides.

Glazebrook, Philip. 1985. *Journey to Kars*. New York: Penguin.

Goethe, Johann Wolfgang von. 1992. *Italian Journey: 1786–1788*. London: Penguin Classics.

Grimble, Arthur. 2010. *A Pattern of Islands*. London: Eland Publishing Ltd.

Hanbury-Tenison, Robin. 2005. *The Oxford Book of Exploration*. New York: Oxford University Press.

Hibbert, Christopher. 1987. *The Grand Tour*. London: Thames Methuen.

Hickson, David J. and Derek S. Pugh. 1995. *Management Worldwide*. London: Penguin Books.

Hiss, Tony. 2001. *In Motion: The Experience of Travel*. Chicago: Planners Press.

Hoggart, Simon. *The Spectator*, 23 October 2010.

Huxley, Aldous. 1985. *Jesting Pilate*. London: Granada Publishing.

Huxley, Aldous. 1989. *Along the Road*. New York: Ecco Press.

Iyer, Pico, ed. 2009. *W. Somerset Maugham: The Skeptical Romancer*. New York: Random House.

Judt, Tony. "The Glory of the Rails," *New York Review of Books*, December 23, 2010 (Vol. LVII, Number 20).

Kieran, Dan. 2012.*The Idle Traveller: The Art of Slow Travel*. Hampshire, UK: A. A. Publishing.

Kinglake, A. W. 1982. *Eothen*. London: Century Publishing.

Kingsley, Charles. 2017. *His Letters and Memories of His Life*. London: Forgotten Books.

Knox, Thomas. 2017. *How to Travel: Hints, Advice, and Suggestons to Travelers by Land and Sea All Over the Globe*. Trieste Publishing.

Lacey, Robert and Danny Danziger. 1999.*The Year 1000: What Life Was Like at the Turn of the 1st Millenium*. New York: Back Bay Books.

Lapham, Lewis, ed. 2009. *Lapham's Quarterly: Travel*. Summer. New York: American Agora Foundation.

Leed, Eric. 1991. *The Mind of the Traveler: From Gilgamesh to Global Tourism*. New York: HarperCollins.

Le Guin, Ursula. 1969. *The Left Hand of Darkness*. New York: Ace Books.

Leki, Ray. "Reality Therapy for Intercultural Training." *Intercultural Management Quarterly*, Fall 2010, Vol. 11, No. 3.

Lewis, Richard. 2003. *The Cultural Imperative: Global Trends in the 21st Century*. Yarmouth, ME: Intercultural Press.

Lewis, Sinclair. 2011. *Dodsworth*. Oxford: Oxford City Press.

MacDonald, Matthew. 2008. *Your Brain: The Missing Manual*. Sebastopol, CA: O'Reilly Media.

Maillart, Ella. 1985. *Turkestan Solo*. London: Century.

Manchester, William. 1992. *A World Lit Only by Fire*. Boston: Little Brown.

Mantel, Hilary. "Last Morning in Al Hamra." *Spectator*, 24 January 1987.

Massingham, Hugh and Pauline Massingham. 1984. *The Englishman Abroad*. London: Alan Sutton.

Maugham, W. Somerset. 1930. *The Gentleman in the Parlour*. London: Heinemann.

Miller, Stuart. 1987. *Understanding Europeans*. Santa Fe, NM: John Muir.

Nees, Greg. 2000. *Germany: Unraveling An Enigma*. Yarmouth, ME: Intercultural Press.

Newby, Eric. 1985. *A Book of Traveller's Tales*. New York. Viking.

Norwich, John Julius. 1985. *A Taste for Travel*. London: MacMillan.

O'Reilly, Sean et al. 2002. *The Road Within*. San Francisco: Traveler's Tales.

Osborne, Roger. 2006. *Civilization: A New History of the Western World*. New York: Regency.

Pells, Richard. 1997. *Not Like Us: How Europeans Have Loved, Hated, and Transformed American Culture Since World War II*. New York: Basic Books.

Platt, Polly. 1995. *French or Foe?: Getting the Most out of Visiting, Living and Working in France* . Skokie, IL: Culture Crossings.

Said, Edward. 1978. *Orientalism*. New York: Random House.

Schiff, Stacy. 1994. *Saint-Exupery: A Biography*. New York: Henry Holt.

Seth, Vikram. 1987. *From Heaven Lake*. New York: Vintage.

Simmons, James C. 1987. *Passionate Pilgrims: English Travelers to the World of the Desert Arabs*. New York: William Morrow.

Smith, Frank. 1978. *Understanding Reading*. New York: Holt, Rinehart and Winston.

Smollett, Tobias. 2010. *Travels through France and Italy*. London: Tauris Parke Paperbacks.

Stark, Freya. 1976. Letters: Volume III: *The Growth of Danger*. London: Compton Russell.

Stark, Freya. 1988. *The Journey's Echo: Selected Travel Writings*. New York: Ecco Press.

Stark, Freya. 1990. *Alexander's Path*. New York. The Overlook Press.

Stark, Freya. 2013. *Perseus in the Wind*. London: Tauris Parke Paperbacks.

Stavans, Ilan and Joshua Ellison. 2015. *Reclaiming Travel*. Durham: Duke University Press.

Steegmuller, Francis, ed. 1987. *Flaubert in Egypt*. Chicago: Academy Chicago Publishers.

Swick, Thomas. 2015. *The Joys of Travel: And Stories That Illuminate Them*. New York: Skyhorse.

Taylor, Edmond. 1964. *Richer by Asia*. New York: Time/Life.

Tharoor, Shashi. 1997. *India: From Midnight to the Millenium and Beyond*. New York: Arcade Publishing.

Theroux, Paul. "Travel Writing: Why I Bother." *New York Times Book Review*, July 30, 1989.

Theroux, Paul. 2006. *The Kingdom by the Sea: A Journey around the Coast of Great Britain*. New York: Mariner.

Theroux, Paul. 2011. *The Tao of Travel: Enlightenments from Lives on the Road*. New York: Houghton Mifflin.

Thomsen, Moritz. 1990. *The Saddest Pleasure: A Journey on Two Rivers*. Minneapolis: Graywolf Press.

Trollope, Frances. 2016. *Paris and the Parisians in 1835*. London: Wallachia Publishers.

Twain, Mark. 1966. *The Innocents Abroad*. New York: Penguin.

Varma, Pavan. 2010. *Becoming Indian: The Unfinished Revolution of Culture and Identity*. New Delhi: Penguin Books India.

Walpole, Horace and Stephen Clarke. 2017. *Selected Letters*. New York: Random House.

Washington Post Book World. January 14, 1990, p. 14.

Watson, Peter. 2005. *Ideas: A History of Thought and Invention, from Fire to Freud*. New York: HarperCollins.

Waugh, Alec. 1989. *Hot Countries*. New York: Paragon House.

Whitfield, Peter. 2011. *Travel: A Literary History*. Oxford: Bodleian Library.

Withey, Lynne. 1997. *Grand Tours and Cook's Tours: A History of Leisure Travel 1750–1915*. New York: William Morrow.

Zeldin, Theodore. 1994. *An Intimate History of Humanity*. New York: Harper Collins.

Zinsser, William, ed. 1991. *They Went: The Art and Craft of Travel Writing*. Boston: Houghton Mifflin.

Permissions

Excerpts on pages 72, 128, 90, and 45: From *Their Heads Are Green, Their Hands Are Blue*, by Paul Bowles. Copyright © 1984 Paul Bowles, used by permission of The Wylie Agency LLC.

Excerpts on pages 94, and 169: From *A Pattern of Islands* by Arthur Grimble. Reprinted by permission of Eland Publishing Ltd. Copyright © Estate of Arthur Grimble 1952.

Jesting Pilate: The Diary of a Journey, by Aldous Huxley. Copyright © 1926, 1953 by Aldous Huxley. Reprinted by Georges Borchardt, Inc. for the Estate of Aldous Huxley. Reproduced from pages 11, 19, 206, 207, and 208.

Extracts on pages 27 and 163, from *Journey to Kars: A Modern Traveller in the Ottoman Lands* by Philip Glazebrook, published by Penguin Books Ltd ©Philip Glazebrook 1985. Reproduced by permission of Sheil Land Associates Ltd.

Extracts on pages 1, 3, 10, 11, 190, and 211: From *A Taste for Travel, An Anthology* by John Julius Norwich, Copyright 1985 by John Julius Normich. Reproduced by permission of Felicity Bryan Literary Agency on behalf of John Julius Norwich.

Map images courtesy of Shutterstock.

Author Biography

Copyright Craig Storti

Craig Storti is a nationally known expert in the field of intercultural communications and cross-cultural adaptation who has lived nearly a quarter of his life abroad. He is the author of several iconic works, including *The Art of Crossing Cultures.* He has over 30-years' experience helping individuals and organizations engage effectively with people from other cultures and diverse backgrounds. Craig is a knowledgeable, practiced traveler–he has touched down in more than 50 countries—and speaks French, Arabic, and Nepali.